GARDENER

▼

D0388637

ALSO BY BARBARA PEARLMAN

Workouts That Work for Women Who Work
Barbara Pearlman's 4-Week Stomach and Waist Shape-Up
Barbara Pearlman's Slendercises
Barbara Pearlman's Dance Excercises

GARDENER'S FITNESS

▼ ▼ ▼ ▼ ▼ ▼ ▼ ▼ ▼

Weeding out the Aches and Pains

▼

Barbara Pearlman

TAYLOR PUBLISHING
Dallas, Texas

Selected information used from: Berlow, Bruce, M.D., "The Hay Fever Harvest," *Flower & Garden*, Aug-Sept 1995, pp. 20–21.

Illustrations by Alison Aldrich

Published by Taylor Publishing Company
1550 West Mockingbird Lane
Dallas, Texas 75235
www.taylorpub.com

Library of Congress Cataloging-in-Publication Data

Pearlman, Barbara.
    Gardener's Fitness : weeding out the aches and pains / Barbara Pearlman.
        p.   cm.
    Includes index.
    ISBN 0-87833-203-0
    1. Gardeners—Health and hygiene. 2. Gardening—Health aspects.
    I. Title.
    RC965.A5P39   1999
    613.7'088'635—dc21   99-11691
                                  CIP

Printed in the United States of America
10 9 8 7 6 5 4 3 2 1

For Stephen

Contents

▼ ▼ ▼ ▼ ▼ ▼ ▼ ▼ ▼ ▼

Acknowledgments

▼▼▼▼▼▼▼▼▼▼▼▼▼▼▼▼▼▼▼▼▼▼▼

I owe my thanks to those who assisted me with this book and inspired me to garden. My appreciation to Jane Dystel, my literary agent, and to all at Taylor who worked on this project. Thanks to dear friends: Lynn Padwe, for your sound advice and for providing photography for the illustrations, and Ciba Vaughan, for your valued support and guidance. To special gardening pals Patti and Jay Rohrlich and Susan Shapiro, thank you for generously sharing your cuttings, computers, and car rides to and from the country. Debbie Brantner Jones, thanks for teaching me so much. For the beauty you have brought to our property, my appreciation to the Mitchell family and to Mark Consolini. Thanks to my son, Aaron, for your encouragement, concern, and delight in nature. Most of all, loving gratitude to my husband, Stephen, who urged me to dig in and write this book.

Introduction
▽▽▽▽▽▽▽▽▽▽▽▽▽

Through the ages, rhapsodic poets and writers have alluded to gardening as a "soul enriching," "body renewing," "spiritually exhilarating" endeavor. I say, let's get down to earth and be real; gardening is an active, contact "sport."

According to the *American Heritage Dictionary* that sits on my desk, sport is "an active pastime or diversion." Sure sounds like gardening to me. And you can bet your begonia it's "active." I mean really, when was the last time you sat still in your garden? If you're not hauling heavy rocks, you're pushing a wheelbarrow, toting tools, dragging the hose, or wacking weeds. You're in perpetual motion, unless of course your idea of gardening is planting a pot of petunias or pansies on your patio.

And let's not hedge the issue. Gardening is not just an *active* sport that can result in sore muscles and aching joints; it's an active *contact* sport. If you really dig in, you're bound to rub against sharp tools, poisonous plants, itchy insects, thorns, slimy slugs. And that's just for starters. All that contact will leave you with a garden-variety of rashes, gashes, bites, and cuts. Not exactly a pretty picture.

So why are we more than willing to forfeit our fingernails and sacrifice our sacroiliacs for the sport of gardening? Simply because there's no earthly pastime quite as heavenly.

In truth, though strenuous and fatiguing (no weakling can prune a vine that has a python grip), the sport of gardening should not wreak havoc on your body, providing that is, you know how to exercise garden sense and smarts. By properly conditioning and preparing yourself for the chores you tackle, and by learning how to move carefully and correctly while you work at your tasks, you can look forward to gardening well beyond your "goldenrod" years.

Just how rigorous gardening can be, and how important it is to train for the sport, became evident to me years ago when I first set my spade in the soil at our newly purchased weekend home in Hillsdale, New York, a sleepy little town in Columbia County.

At that time, the allure and attraction of owning a weekend retreat, at least for me, was rest and relaxation. Not only did my mind need to chill out from the chaos of Manhattan (where I worked a long and arduous week as an exercise consultant), but my body needed time-out. Well, my mind got just what it needed—serenity and seclusion. As for my body, that's a whole different story.

The house we purchased was built on speculation, and it sat vacant for just over a year—for good reason. It was remarkably devoid of character, both inside and out. A very modest Dutch colonial, it was hardly the quaint, sprawling, old farmhouse I longed to own. But it fit our budget, and it was the absolute final house my husband, Stephen, was willing to look at after having begrudgingly traipsed through other people's bedrooms, bathrooms, closets, and attics for eight months. "It's this one or no one," he assertively stated as we stood on the non-lawn on a windy, mid-March afternoon in the late seventies. And so we bought it.

Remote and isolated, the house sat on a slight incline and faced a meandering dirt road that gave a bit of charm to what was an open but otherwise undistinguished view. There were no lawns, no foundation plantings (the builder went broke), no mature trees to soften the lines. In fact, there were no trees in front whatsoever. The sparse growth that bordered both sides of the house obviously provided lunch for the deer, evident by piles of poop planted about.

Unlike the front, the acreage behind the house was utterly overgrown and grubby. Yes, there was a great deal growing in the back, with poison ivy heading a long list of untouchables and undesirables. Vines strangled many of the deciduous trees, and dense, dead pine limbs obscured the sunlight. The grounds cried out for a green thumb; but more important, a strong back.

The picture, however, was not entirely dismal. A winding brook ran down from the hilltop to the base of the property, and a stone wall stood proud, having survived the passing of time beautifully intact. As for the birdsongs that reverberated through the woods, they were utterly glorious—all of which gave me reason to believe there might be hope for this little plot of potential paradise.

So, after weeks of settling in and furnishing the empty rooms with bare necessities found at local shops, auctions, and tag sales, I was resolved, once mud season was over, to tackle the grounds and transform at least a small portion of the eight acres into my own little Sissinghurst. Not only was the idea utterly naive and unrealistic, but the undertaking was also backbreaking—exactly what my weekends were not supposed to be.

During that initial spring and summer, I nursed a garden-variety of inflictions and irritations ranging from bugs in the eye to elbow tendinitis. On Monday mornings, there I was lying face down on a massage table, hoping that Anat, the lady with the miracle hands, could put my body back (and especially my back) into working order.

Was it really possible that I wasn't prepared for the rigors of gardening? *Me*, the very person described as "slender as a reed, supple as a rubber band" in a *New York Times* article about "Manhattan's Fitness Guru." *Me*, who supposedly was in good shape from years of working in my field (but obviously not in the fields).

As I toiled in the soil and crawled around in the trenches those first few months, acquainting myself with muscles I never knew I had, I couldn't help wondering: How on earth does someone who's out of shape manage to keep a garden in shape?

And that's just when, why, and how the idea for this book took root. It became very apparent to me that training for the sport of gardening really does makes sense. And it makes sense even if you are fit and in enviable shape. That's because the demands gardening places on the body are unique. Sure, you might have lung and leg power from jogging or biking, for instance, but that doesn't necessarily mean you're conditioned for the lugging and tugging, not to mention the crawling around on all fours, that gardening demands.

I confess it took many years before I actually sat down to write *Gardener's Fitness*. Despite urgings from friends and clients who garden, the timing was always a problem. During the winter, when I had the time to write, the aches, pains, and heartbreaks that gardening evokes and provokes were a mere memory. Then, with the very first sign of spring, there was no sign of me— not at my desk, that is. The last place I wanted to plant myself was in front of a computer! I wanted to be back in my garden. And so I was.

Way back then, when my fixation for gardening took hold, I not only recognized how tough and sweaty the sport can be (providing *you* do the grunt work), but I also realized, having met my fair share of passionate maniacs, just how obsessive gardeners can be.

When gardeners have a chore to accomplish, it becomes nothing short of a categorical imperative; we get down on our hands and knees and practically bend over backwards to shape up our beds and borders. The problem is, many gardeners are not particularly comfortable on their hands and knees, and still more can't manage to bend over backwards. Well, not easily, that is.

For this very reason, I wrote *Gardener's Fitness* to help you condition, maintain, and care for your most important tool—your body. Granted, books on every aspect of gardening have been written. I know because I've been collecting and reading them for years. Yet, searching the shelves at libraries and bookstores, I failed to unearth a practical, easy-to-follow conditioning and fitness primer for gardeners. And, in truth, had I not finally transplanted myself from the garden to the house, this book, which you might say cross-pollinates my profession with my passion, might never have seen the light of day either.

No, this is not another how-to-garden book filled with creative concepts and complex horticultural advice; I leave that to the real experts. This book is about how to garden comfortably, safely, and sanely so that you can play at the sport of gardening for years to come, whether you're a seasoned gardener or a mere rookie.

Within *Gardener's Fitness*, you will find conditioning exercises to train and ready you for the season, as well as movement techniques and postural guidance for lifting, pushing, hauling, squatting, and whatever else you have to do to get the job done. I've also included simple, on-the-spot stretches that you can do almost effortlessly—right in the garden—to relax weary muscles and restore energy. And there's even a selection of soothing, therapeutic stretches that benefit from warm water, easily done in the bath or shower while you de-grime at the end of the day. In addition, the book offers beneficial damage control strategies and remedies (mostly natural) for the likes of sunburn and bug bites.

Over the years, my gardening pals have been a source of inspiration and information (not to mention plant matter). They have entertained and enlightened me with gardening sagas and stories and have shared their time-tested tactics, be it a method to take the ivy off the house or the itch out of poison ivy. Although we might not all agree on what best deters the deer, or which is the most drought-resistant perennial for our particular zone, we all agree that it makes sense to weed the aches and pains out of gardening.

I have also had the good fortune to learn gardening survival tactics from men and women, young and old, who over the past few years have participated in my workshops on gardening fitness. And I have learned from kind and caring souls

▼

who work at nurseries in the Berkshires; they have guided me through a multitude of horticultural crises and calamities.

But above all, from years of gardening, I have learned about nature—human nature (mine to be exact). My garden has truly been a training ground, not only for my body but for my head—for my "mental muscle." That's because gardening demands far more than just physical conditioning; you really have to be mentally "flexible" to manage the headaches and heartaches Mother Nature bats in your direction. Your hopes, plans, and dreams for your garden can literally be blown away (or eaten away!) overnight.

Sure, you can compete with the "lady in control," but she ultimately gets the last licks. You really can't be a control freak and garden happily. After many years, I have finally allowed my garden to rescue me from rigidity. No longer do I feel compelled to create utter neatness and order in my garden—or in my life. "Organized chaos" is more like it, and I like it more that way. Nor do I have to be constantly moving and doing in my garden—or in my life. Today, I actually can (and do) stay put, seated quietly on a tree stump near the brook or on the front lawn under our now majestic oak. I'm perfectly content to allow my mind to drift and my body to rest. No

longer am I quite as obsessed (I'm not totally cured!) to work at the sport of gardening; with the passing of each year, it's more about "play" and "amusement." And because, at long last, I am somewhat less maniacal about this passion, my garden has become more nourishing, exactly what it should be.

What was formerly an uninviting, scrubby property is today a source of beauty, pleasure, and enormous pride. Is my garden a top contender for a garden tour? Not at all; it's blooming with mistakes and I'm learning all the time. There are colors that conflict and plants that are actually gaudy. Tall, back-of-the-border (according to the experts) specimens grow undisturbed in territory that should belong (according to the experts) to the little guys.

But that's perfectly fine with me, because my garden is one place where, finally, at the age of fifty-six, I can do as I please. I can break the rules if I wish and garden simply for the pure joy of it; and I do—without the fear of penalties.

And that's just one of many reasons I absolutely adore the "sport" of gardening. For most of us, daily life imposes an endless array of rules, restrictions, and regulations. But in the garden, you don't have to stand up to the plate and be accounted for. You can do exactly as you wish and feel good about it. That is, if you remember to bend your knees!

ONE

Don't Let Your Body Go to Seed

There's no worming out of it. Though supremely satisfying, utterly absorbing and thoroughly addictive, gardening can also be tough and tiring, particularly if your garden is in better shape than you are. No, you really can't expect your body to spring into action when spring arrives, not if you plant yourself on the couch all winter, watching gardening videos. Sure, once the weather beckons, you may be ready to begin all the exciting projects that percolated in your mind, but believe me, it's not your mind that will perform the grunt work.

The sport of gardening requires strength, stamina, and flexibility, none of which, I can assure you, come from leafing through seed catalogs. That's why it's important to do the groundwork, to strengthen and condition the "body zones" that really get a workout when you're out working in the garden. I'm specifically referring to your arms, knees, hands, and, above all, your back.

The exercises from this section that you choose to practice (those that best fit your particular needs) should be based on several factors: the present shape you're in, the gardening tasks and chores (strenuous or simple) you take on, and the signals you get from your body after a day of work. If, for example, knee discomfort frequently results from squatting when you plant bulbs or when you weed, it obviously makes sense to strengthen and thus better protect your knees by conditioning the appropriate muscles.

Knee conditioning indirectly results from strengthening the quadriceps (the front of your thighs) and hamstrings (the back of your thighs), which is exactly what the exercises on pages 35–37 are designed to do. By practicing these movements, you can and will add considerably to your knees' capacity to ward off stress.

1

Or once you strengthen your arms with the appropriate exercises, tasks such as preparing a new flower bed or turning the compost will be easier to manage. And there's a bonus to toning your arms: When they're strong, other areas, such as your neck and shoulders, will not be taxed to compensate for weak arms.

As for the exercises designed for improving your hand strength and dexterity, they will pay off, for sure, when you're deadheading, digging, weeding, or handling tools, power or otherwise. In fact, if you suffer from osteoarthritis in the finger joints, these exercises are important to include in your shape-up routine.

Or perhaps weak abdominal muscles cause your back to protest when you haul a heavy bag of manure from the garage to the yard, or when you push the wheelbarrow to your hilltop cutting garden. (I know you're wondering why you put it there in the first place.) Of all the aches and pains common to gardeners, backaches win hands down; that's because so many tasks and chores require spinal strength and stability. So unless your back never gives you trouble (while or after you garden), the back strengthening and stretching exercises should be included in your training program.

In selecting the appropriate conditioning exercises to ready you for your tasks, I not only considered which body zones are most used and abused while one works in the garden but also considered the contorted, distorted positions one often gets into—willingly or not.

With utter enthusiasm and total abandon, gardeners perform acrobatic feats (some of which temporarily invalid us) while attempting to beautify their beds and borders. (In truth, by Sunday evening in late summer, the only bed I can relate to is the queen-size one in my bedroom!) Be it tiptoeing through the tulips during a flashlight raid on slugs, or poking around on all fours to strategically place a soaker hose that has a mind of its own, we often end up with our ends up.

For this reason, I've included some easy but effective flexibility exercises that are designed to stretch your calves, hamstrings, hip flexors, and back extensor muscles. When tight, these muscles not only cause your back to overwork but also limit your range of motion, which could result in injury, not only to yourself but to the plants you inadvertently trample due to lack of flexibility!

Let's take a for instance: Your hamstrings are tight, you bend over to lift a bag of fertilizer, and bingo—your back goes into spasm. Improved flexibility will not only keep injury at bay but will also enable you to accomplish tasks that involve bending, lifting, reaching, and so forth with far more ease and agility.

(Even worse than slugs in the garden is a klutz!)

For each body zone of concern, I've included a set of safe and effective strengthening exercises. The movements I've selected are basic, so don't be concerned that you need to be athletic (or balletic) to manage them. The object of this program is to prepare you for gardening, not the Olympics.

No one knows better than you exactly which zones need attention. That's because you, and only you, get the signals from your body when you're working in your garden (and afterward). With this selection of exercises, you can design a program for your specific needs. You can select exercises from only one or two parts of this conditioning program. Or you can choose to do exercises from each part to derive a more complete and overall conditioning. The choice is yours.

Unless you find it excessive, in which case you can reduce the repetitions I've called for, begin with the suggested numbers for each exercise. Once you are able to do them with control and good form, you can increase the numbers, adding no more than two additional repetitions per exercise, per week. (You will be surprised what a difference adding even a mere two will make.)

Doing the movements correctly, with good focus and form, is far more important than performing endless, mindless repetitions. And that holds true for doing any of the exercises in the book, even the ones I recommend that you do right in the garden to "de-stress" tired muscles.

Try, if you can, to practice the conditioning exercises *regularly*, because consistency is important for progress. The flexibility exercises, which actually take little time (but which should not be rushed), are most effective when practiced daily. As for the conditioning exercises, you will benefit most by doing them four or five days a week.

When practicing the exercises, stay focused on moving correctly and well. For instance, how far away from the floor are your knees when doing the flexibility stretch for your low back extensor muscles (page 9)? Does it feel different (easier, harder) from the last time you practiced it? What I'm basically saying is this: Don't put your body on automatic pilot. By allowing your mind to wander and soar, you could easily end up with sore muscles.

Some of the flexibility enhancers may feel uncomfortable at first, especially if your range of motion is limited, due to age, injury, arthritis, or simply because you're out of shape. Muscles that are awakened for the first time, or for the first time in a long time, may protest until they learn to enjoy being stretched. So don't force any of the movements; if you reach a point of painful resistance, stop. There's a big difference between a good pain and a bad pain. Good pain is the pain of restoring elasticity to a tight muscle; bad pain warns of incipient injury.

Remember as well, proper breathing is crucial to exercising correctly. Never hold your breath; this deprives your muscles of necessary oxygen. If you find that you are holding your breath while doing any of the exercises, you're probably working with too much intensity and need to relax a bit. Try to inhale (through your nose) as you move into a stretch and exhale (through your mouth) as you hold the stretch. An easy way to focus on the exhalation is to make a soft "s" sound, like a hiss, as in "s-s-s-salvia" or "s-s-s-sedum."

As for correct breath control, in general while you practice these exercises, try to exhale through your mouth during the effort phase of any movement (exertion) and inhale through your nose as you move into the relaxation phase. For most exercises, this involves exhaling as you lift (that is, your torso, leg, arm) and inhaling as you lower your limb(s) or torso.

Before practicing the exercises you select for your personalized program, spend a few minutes warming up. For the brief warm-up, walk briskly (or jog) in place while swinging your arms for three or four minutes at most. The warm-up does not require fancy footwork, nor does it have to be strenuous or make you perspire. A mild warm-up simply prepares your body by raising the temperature of the muscles and lubricating the joints, making them less susceptible to damage or injury.

And speaking of warming up, it's really wise to do so *before* you garden as well. Taking a few minutes (and that's all you need) to limber up prior to "digging in" is time well-spent. For a short and simple warm-up, you can use some or all of the flexibility enhancers found at the end of this section.

Before I leave the house, no matter how eager I am to get into the garden, I always take a few minutes to stretch my lower back muscles. One exercise that works particularly well for me is the knee rock (page 89). I do this back-relaxing movement prior to gardening and afterward as well. In fact, on mornings when my back feels stiff from having done too much heavy-duty work the day before, I actually do a minute or two of gentle knee rocking before I even get out of bed.

And speaking of mornings, if you're like me, in your glory and in your garden at the crack of dawn, try if you can to exercise a bit of restraint. Delay doing really strenuous tasks until your muscles are fully awake and alert. Deadheading at sunrise is sane, but removing and moving stumps is not.

▽ ▽ ▽ ▽ ▽   TIP   ▽ ▽ ▽ ▽ ▽

What to do when you're outside with filthy hands and the nearest sink is on the other side of the back door? Hang soap near the garden hose spigot. This way cleanup is handy. Just slip a bar into the foot of an old panty hose and tie the fabric into a knot. Then hang the soap hose by your garden hose.

Because your body is a precious tool (parts not easily replaced), it obviously makes good garden sense to ready this tool *prior* to peak season. Ideally, you should begin your preseason training at least eight weeks before the first spring bulbs make their debut. However, if you neglect to do so, only to find yourself knee deep in soil, unable to flex anything including your green thumb, it's not too late. Your body, like your garden, is a work in progress.

Your Back

In Hillsdale, when my gardening "comrades" gather at a party (garden or otherwise), we invariably end up discussing how to cope with the agony that bonds us. You guessed it because chances are you've had it! Back pain. It's the gardener's bugaboo. Unless your back is made of steel (in which case, you probably can't get into all the contorted positions gardening calls for), at some point during the season, your back is bound to protest.

Just think about it, from early spring when you begin to clean up the garden (not to mention the garage) to late fall when you put it (hopefully not yourself) to bed, your back is constantly called upon and put upon. And it's not just the heavy work that taxes your back; even lighter tasks, when sustained for extended periods, can cause your back to complain.

Although I do agree that back discomfort can be relieved by the likes of ice packs and ibuprofen, the very best defense against back pain is a good offense, which means strong abdominal muscles. To a great extent, your abdominal muscles are responsible for your back's health, comfort, and mobility, be it when you're bent over planting hundreds of bulbs or crawling on your hands and knees across your rose garden evicting Japanese beetles.

The importance of the abdominal muscles center on their role in protecting your back, specifically your disks, from permanent injury. And that's exactly why it's so important that if your back tends to give you trouble when you garden, you faithfully, carefully, and correctly strengthen your abdominal muscles. When these muscles are strong and toned, your back will be better able to manage the demands placed on it, whether you're lifting a bulky bag of lime or hauling the hose up the hill.

Now that's not to say if your abdominal muscles are strong, you will be forever immune to back pain. No way. Even the hardiest among us experience occasional fatigue and discomfort, whether from overloading the wheelbarrow or simply nonstop gardening without a break. But your recovery rate, as well as your ability to protect your spine, will be enhanced if your abdominals are well conditioned.

Although they do not actually connect with the back, the abdominals form a remarkable package of four layers of overlapping, crisscrossing fibers: the rectus abdominis, strongest and closest to the surface, which runs from the ribs down to the pelvis; the internal and external obliques, which weave diagonally from opposite sides; and the transversalis abdominis muscles, which extend from side to side and, essentially, from front to back across the abdominal cavity. In essence, these muscles act as "guy wires" to keep your back in line. If the wires are weak, their hold on the spine cannot be sufficiently protective.

Additionally, strong abdominals protect not only your back muscles from overworking but your leg muscles as well. If, for instance, you bend over to pull out a stubborn weed or to pick up a tool when your back lacks flexibility and strength, your hamstrings, as well as your knees, have to overwork to compensate.

So too, Mother Nature (aka "gravity" in nongardening circles) will drag the contents of the abdominal cavity forward and downward, increasing the natural curve or arch in your lower back if your abdominals are weak. This creates a swayback that in turn causes other muscles to stretch and tighten to compensate. And that's exactly why gardening-related back problems often lead to pain in the buttock and hip areas as well.

The good news is, like clematis and honeysuckle, muscles are trainable; they can be made looser or tighter with exercise. In terms of your abdominals, you certainly do not want to loosen them. In fact, they are one group of muscles you never want to loosen. Flaccid abdominals cannot provide adequate balance and support for your back, which is what you really need when you work at strenuous chores.

In addition to the abdominal-strengthening exercises (numbers 8–12), I've included back flexibility stretches that target three areas: the extensors (which run along the length of your lower spine), hip flexors, and hamstrings, all of which contribute to the fitness and strength of the lower back. Strong extensor muscles, for instance, work in partnership with your abdominals to support your lower back when you lift a shrub out of the ground or carry stepping stones to a newly prepared bed.

To derive full benefit from this brief back care program, I recommend that you do one flexibility stretch for each of the three abovementioned areas. Then proceed with the pelvic tilt, which strengthens the lower back, followed by at least two abdominal strengtheners out of the five. The abdominal strengtheners appear in order of difficulty.

"For the past forty years, I have broken my nails, my back, and sometimes my heart in the practical pursuit of my favorite occupation."
EDITH SACKVILLE-WEST

BACK FLEXIBILITY

#1 Hip Flexor Stretch

Position: Stand with one foot ahead of the other, keeping both feet flat on the floor and parallel, toes pointed forward. Assume a stride that is challenging, but not too wide. Relax your arms at your sides or rest your hands on your forward thigh.

Movement: Slowly lunge forward on the front foot until the knee is slightly bent. Push your hips forward by tucking your pelvis under. You should feel tension in the quadriceps of the front leg and the inner thigh, calf, and hip flexors of the back leg. Hold the position for 30 seconds, then repeat on the other leg.

Note: Make certain that you do not overbend the forward knee.

#2 Hip Flexor Stretch

Position: Sit with your legs extended forward and your knees flat, but not hyperextended (locked).

Movement: Gradually reach forward for your toes, bending from your hips rather than from your waist. Keep your abdominals in and hold the stretch for thirty seconds.

"Life begins the day you start a garden."
CHINESE PROVERB

#3 Hamstring Stretch

Position: Lie on your back with your right leg bent, foot flat on the floor. Bring your left knee toward your chest and hold it with both hands behind the thigh.

Movement: Extend the left leg toward the ceiling, foot flexed. In this extended position, gently draw the leg toward your chest. Hold thirty seconds. Lower the leg and repeat on the other leg.

#4 Pelvic Arch (back extensors)

Position: Lie on your back with your head resting in your hands. Place your feet on the floor, parallel and hip-width apart.

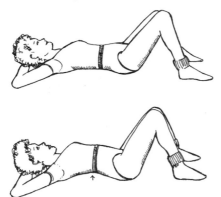

Movement: Alternately flatten then arch the small of your back by first

▼ ▼ ▼ ▼ ▼ **TIP** ▼ ▼ ▼ ▼ ▼

If your basketball has deflated and you've retired your high-tops, there's still life for the hoop. A garbage can plus the hoop are all the supplies you need to tidy up the garden tools scattered about the garage. (If you don't have a hoop, check out local tag or garage sales.) Remove the net from the hoop. With screws, fasten the hoop to the wall of the garage or tool shed about four feet above the floor. Set a large trash can under the hoop and place your tall tools, such as rakes and hoes, through it and in the can. Without any hoopla, your tools will stand upright and tidy.

contracting the muscles of the lower back, then releasing them. Keep the motion fluid and slow. Repeat the flattening/arching sequence six times. Exhale to contract, inhale to arch.

Note: This movement is effective for increasing spinal mobility.

#5 Backup (back extensors)

Position: Begin on your hands and knees, hands directly underneath your shoulders, knees directly underneath your hips. Do not lock your elbows. Rest the tops of your feet on the floor. Tuck your chin and let your abdominals relax just slightly. (The position of your body is like a table; your back is flat and your arms and legs are like table legs.)

Movement: Contract your abdominal muscles and slowly, taking four counts, arch your back upward so that you feel a stretch through the entire length of your back. Hold for four counts. Then, slowly, without allowing your abdominals to sag or your back to make a concave arch, take four counts to return to the "tabletop" position. Repeat eight times. Exhale to arch, inhale to flatten.

Note: It is possible to make your body move into the arched position without using your abdominal muscles: you can just lift up your rib cage and tighten your buttocks to hunch your back. But the exercise is only effective if you use your abdominal muscles to do the work. (This exercise can be done right in the garden to relax your back when

you're working on your hands and knees.)

"Gardening takes a plot of land, a hoe and willing muscles."
RICHARDSON WRIGHT

#6 Knee Roll (back extensors)
Position: Lie on your back with your knees and feet together; your heels should not be directly under your knees but slightly in front of them. Extend your arms at shoulder level, palms down.

Movement: First pull in your abdominal muscles, then slowly roll your knees to the right while turning your head to the left. (Make certain to anchor yourself with your left shoulder; it should not lift off the floor.) Hold for two counts, then bring your knees back to the center while

pulling in your abdominals. Repeat the roll to the left. Inhale as you roll, exhale as you return to the center. Repeat the side to side motion twelve times total.

Note: Depending on your flexibility, your knees may or may not reach the floor; do not strain to lower them. By doing this exercise slowly and with control, you will be able to focus on keeping your abdominal muscles pulled in, which is important for back protection.

#7 Pelvic Tilt

Position: Lie on the floor with your knees bent, feet flat and hip-width apart and parallel. Relax your arms at your sides or rest your head in your hands. Do not overbend your knees.

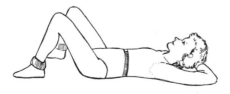

Movement: Gently contract your abdominal and buttock muscles as you lift your hips and buttocks slightly off the floor. (Do not lift your waist.) Hold for four slow counts, then, keeping your abdomi-

nals contracted, slowly lower to the starting position. Inhale on the lift, exhale on the release. Repeat 10 times.

Note: Not only will this exercise strengthen your abdominals, but it will also strengthen your gluteus maximus muscles (buttock muscles), which, when in good condition, prevent excessive lumbar spinal curve (swayback).

ABDOMINAL STRENGTHENERS

#8 Tilt and Slide

Position: Lie on your back with your knees bent and your feet parallel and hip-width apart. Place your hands behind your head or relax them at your sides.

Movement: Contract your abdominals and press the small of your back into the floor. Take four counts to slowly slide both legs forward, trying to straighten them as much as possible while maintaining the abdominal contraction. Stop at the point when you can no longer keep your back flat. Time a slow exhalation to the sliding motion. Repeat six times.

▼

▽ ▽ ▽ ▽ ▽ **TIP** ▽ ▽ ▽ ▽ ▽

One-fifth of our nation's air pollution is caused by gas-powered lawn machinery, according to the Environmental Protection Agency. In fact, just thirty minutes of mowing creates more pollution than three hours of driving in your car. Reel mowers were originally advertised in the 1830s in England as "an amusing, useful and healthy exerciser for the country gentleman." And in fact, they get the job done for less money while giving the pusher a mini-aerobic workout.

Among the best exercises for strengthening the abdominal muscles are sit-ups and "crunches," which involve bending or flexing your spine by moving your upper body, lower body, or both at the same time, a small way toward your middle. Done correctly, these movements firm your abdominals and lift them upward and inward. But before you practice any of the following abdominal strengthening exercises, a few tips:

► For crunches to be effective, do not rush through them; in lieu of muscle strength, fast crunches depend on momentum to swing you through the movement, which is not what you want to achieve.

► Avoid pulling on your neck with your hands as you lift. Use your fingertips to support your head (do not interlace your fingers) by placing your thumbs at the base of your head, on the upper neck.

► Always exhale through your mouth during the exertion phase (lifting) and inhale through your nose during the relaxation phase (lowering).

► After several repetitions, your abdominals may begin to push out, it's only natural. When this occurs, stop momentarily to contract them once again before you resume the exercise.

► When lifting your upper body, avoid thrusting your head forward, which strains the neck.

#9 Curl-Up

Position: Lie on your back with your knees bent, feet flat and hip-width apart and parallel. Rest your hands on your thighs.

Movement: Pull in your abdominals as you raise your shoulder blades off the floor and slide your hands toward your knees. Take two counts to lift and two counts to lower. Exhale with each lift. Repeat twelve times.

Note: To avoid straining your neck, do not bob your head up and down; keep your chin tucked.

#10 Crunch

Position: Lie on your back, knees bent, feet parallel and hip-width apart. Place your fingers behind your head, thumbs behind your ears for neck support. Hold your elbows wide apart and tuck your chin slightly toward your chest, leaving space for an imaginary orange between your chin and chest. (If your chin is lifted too high, the orange will slip; too low and you will have orange juice!) Contract your abdominals toward your spine by tilting your pelvis slightly upward.

Movement: Curl up and forward so that your head, neck, and shoulders lift off the floor in one unit. Hold the lifted position for two counts, then lower slowly. Repeat twelve times.

Note: On the upward motion, imagine your center being weighted down, which will keep your lower back flat and grounded.

#11 Crossover Crunch (oblique abdominal strengthener)

Position: Lie on your back with your right heel resting on your left knee. Place your hands behind your head, thumbs behind your ears. Do not interlace your fingers. Open your elbows wide. Pull your abdominals toward your spine and tilt your pelvis slightly upward.

Movement: Lift your head, neck, and shoulder blades off the floor as you move your left elbow toward your right knee by smoothly twisting from your middle. Repeat ten times, then repeat to the other side.

"If gardeners had been developing from the beginning of the world by natural selection, they would have evolved most probably into some kind of invertebrate. After all, for what purpose has a gardener a back?"

KAREL ČAPEK

---

12 Roll Down

Position: Sit on the floor with your knees bent, arms extended in front at chest level, and hands clasped together.

Movement: Pull in your abdominals, lower your chin, and slowly roll back touching one vertebra at a time to the floor until your lower back is resting on the floor. Time an exhalation of breath to the rolling back

motion. Aim for maximum smoothness and rounding. Then, continuing to keep your back rounded, inhale and slowly return to the original position. Repeat slowly ten times.

Note: When done correctly, this exercise will stretch the back and tighten the abdominals, working them together. To challenge your abdominals still more, once you have managed the halfway roll back with control, you can then practice rolling all the way down to the floor.

DAMAGE CONTROL: BACK SPASM AND FATIGUE

Okay, you've done everything possible to strengthen and stretch your back muscles, but late one afternoon, while you're crawling on your hands and knees, reaching to weed the mint that's invaded the basil (yet again), you feel it coming on. It's the Back Attack!

Few gardeners can report, even if they are in the good shape, that they never experience the garden-variety of low back pain. So, what should you do when a back spasm occurs? For starters, listen to your body, which translates as: stop gardening, even if you're in the midst of a must-do project. Without sounding too horticulturally cute, it makes good sense to nip a back spasm in the bud.

Head for the house, strip out of your dirty clothes, and lie down on your back (knees bent) on an ice pack or cold pack placed directly under the spot where you feel the pain. Because your back is feeling vulnerable, it's best not to lie on a hard wooden floor but instead on a rug or carpet. And you want to leave the pack (and yourself) in place for fifteen to twenty minutes.

"What a man needs in gardening is a cast-iron back, with a hinge on it."
CHARLES DUDLEY WARNER

Why the ice pack in lieu of a heating pad? For the most part, back pain (particularly lower back pain) is nearly always caused by spasm of the back muscles; ice slows transmission time in the pain-conducting nerve fibers. What it actually does is slow down the nerve's ability to conduct painful stimuli (a process called reflex vasoconstriction), thereby breaking the vicious cycle of muscle spasm-pain-muscle spasm. It also causes the blood vessels to constrict and retard the leakage of fluid into the surrounding tissues.

This process is then followed by the opposite phenomenon, reflex vasodilation, which means that the blood vessels now dilate or expand spontaneously, allowing more blood to flow to the muscle in spasm. Because much of the pain of muscle spasm comes from a relatively low supply of blood (ischmia), this new supply, with the oxygen it carries, also helps to reduce the pain.

It's a good idea to always keep a cold pack handy in your freezer. Commercial packs, sold in drugstores, can be chilled so that the gel inside remains cold for a long time while it's applied to the area. In addition to the store-bought variety, I also keep a bag of frozen peas in the freezer, a more, shall we say, vegetarian approach to the ice pack. The peas mold easily around an injured area, such as a wrist or ankle. Corn kernels or carrot cubes will work, too!

There are numerous ways to apply ice. A plastic bag filled with ice chips is one method; however, a thin towel should be used to protect your skin. You can also fill several paper cups with water, then freeze them for use as an "ice massage." When it comes time to massage a painful area, just tear the paper away from the sides of the cup, exposing the ice but leaving the bottom paper portion to hold. Then you slowly massage the area of injury with short overlapping strokes. But be sure to keep the ice moving, otherwise you could slightly freeze and injure surface tissues.

As a matter of fact, ice must always be used with caution and care, in whatever form. According to Dr. Willibald Nagler, Physiatrist-in-Chief at the New York Hospital Cornell Medical Center, ice should be applied for fifteen to twenty minutes but not longer. After that time, it will have no beneficial physiological effect. Actually, the greatest benefit from ice, according to Nagler, accrues after twelve to fourteen minutes, but it's best to keep it applied for twenty minutes to make sure that you achieve maximum cooling beneath the surface of the skin.

Heat, too, increases blood flow by dilating the blood vessels and by helping to deliver oxygen and carry off waste products. So heat is the line of attack for back muscles that are simply sore or just overworked. However, it's not as effective as ice for muscle spasm; the combination of vasoconstriction followed by vasodilation provided by ice is much more powerful, says Nagler.

But remember, heat should never be used during the acute phase of any muscle, tendon, or ligament injury. It will promote the leakage of fluid from the blood vessels and lead to increased, rather than decreased, swelling, according to Nagler.

Okay, so there you are, lying on your back, which is in "deep freeze," wishing you were in your sun-drenched garden tending to your peas, not lying on them. What else do you do? You breathe! That's right. That's all you have to do, nothing more. Slow, deep breathing can help relax tight muscles and reduce some of the anxiety resulting from back pain. You might even listen to some music while you lie there "on ice," anything but "Tiptoe Through the Tulips," which would only rub it in.

To do the deep breathing, simply inhale slowly through your nose, taking all the time you can, without straining. You then want to exhale slowly through softly pursed lips, trying to prolong the exhalation for as long as you can, again without straining. In fact, when exhaling, just try to make a very soft sound, not a loud, forceful blow. And you really should devote a minimum of five minutes to this breathing exercise. Better yet, you might continue to do it for the entire time your back is getting the "cold treatment."

But there's still more to be done, once the "icing" is completed. No, you're not going to race into the gar-den to finish what you left undone, particularly if it's a chore that taxes your back. Instead, you want to remain on the floor so you can do one simple but effective limbering movement designed to loosen your muscles rather than stretch them.

The exercise that I'm suggesting prevents the back muscles from tightening further and is different from the stretching exercises I rec-ommended earlier in this section. The reason is that muscles in spasm should *never* be stretched; it only makes the spasm worse.

This exercise is done by lying on your back with your knees bent and your feet flat. You slowly bring your left knee up toward your chest as far as possible, without using your hands. You then return your foot to the floor with the knee still bent. Next, you slowly slide the heel along the floor until the leg is straight. In this position, you gently roll the leg from side to side before slowly and carefully sliding it back to the start-ing bent-knee position. Naturally, you then repeat the same leg sequence with the other leg. Try to do three or four repetitions with each leg.

You may also want to take a mild pain reliever, such as Advil or Tylenol, if you're really uncomfort-able, which should reduce some of the discomfort from the spasm. During the first day, you should repeat the ice-exercise sequence a minimum of four or five times. If the spasm is really severe, hourly application of ice is a good idea.

In two or three days, the painful muscle spasm should have subsided significantly. However, if in the first forty-eight hours your back does not begin to improve or gets worse, it may be necessary to consult a physician.

If, on the other hand, your back is not in spasm but instead simply feels fatigued after gardening for hours, it's not a bad idea to lie down and give your back a well-deserved rest, even if it's just for fifteen or twenty minutes. Because heat works well on overworked muscles, now would be the time to lie on a heating pad. A warm bath is another option. In both cases, the heat should not be so excessive that it burns your skin.

There's yet another way to protect a vulnerable back besides wearing a corset (see page 68) when doing strenuous chores: keep your back muscles warm and insulated when you garden on less than ideal days. If you're putting your garden to bed in late fall or cleaning up your grounds in early spring, and the weather is cold and damp, keep your back protected by wearing layers of clothing.

A flannel sweatshirt or tightly woven woolen sweater, covered by a lightweight, nylon shell, allows for ease of motion while protecting your back from cold and wind. As a matter of fact, on damp, cool days, wearing layers, instead of a bulky jacket for instance, will allow you to move more easily and comfortably. Then, once your body heats up, you can shed a layer or two.

For added insulation when I work in the yard in cold weather, I often wear a thin layer of silk underwear (from the L. L. Bean Catalog). Not only does silk feel wonderful next to my skin (it's like having a second skin), but it's lightweight and doesn't add bulk.

Gardeners, as you know, are forever discussing the state and condition of their beds. But one bed can have considerable effect on the state of your back, and thus indirectly on the state of your garden; that's the one you sleep in. Take my word for it, if you want to garden all day, you really need to get a comfortable, good night's sleep.

For sure, sleeping in a soft bed is not a back healthy choice. Instead, you should opt for a firm mattress or, if the mattress is not adequately supportive, place a plywood board between the bed base and the mattress. These boards can generally be purchased at bedding supply stores, or you can have one cut to your specifications at a local lumber yard.

As for the best sleeping position for back care and comfort: if you sleep on your back, place a pillow under your knees so that they can remain slightly bent. A flexed knee position reduces stress on the lower back. If, however, you prefer sleeping on your side (a better choice), you should use a single pillow under your neck so that your head remains properly aligned, not higher than your spine. (Mounds of pillows wreck the neck!) Try to keep your knees bent in this position as well. In fact, you might want to place a pillow between your knees for added back protection.

Speaking of beds and rest, there's no evidence that bed rest works best for gardening-induced back pain. Not only is bed rest ineffective for most people, in most cases, according to the experts I consulted, it only leads to deterioration of the muscular system. Studies overwhelmingly favor "sensible" movement and activity for back discomfort. But mind you, "sensible" does not mean digging up a fifty-pound hydrangea and moving it single-handedly across the yard.

"Old gardeners never die, they just spade away."

GENE ROTHERT

Your Arms

Raking leaves, winding up the hose, double-digging, turning the compost, and other chores that require arm strength will be easier to manage and less taxing if your arms are toned and conditioned. In fact, weak forearm muscles actually contribute to tennis elbow.

Why, you ask, am I making a racket about tennis elbow in the garden? Because millions of people who don't play tennis suffer from it and many of them are—that's right—gardeners! Not only is the term "faulted," but it's misleading and inaccurate because sufferers do not have pain inside their elbow; they feel it on the outside of the joint just above the elbow crease.

Pain appears at that spot because it's the very point at which the major muscles in the forearm are anchored to the upper-arm bone by a tendon, the point where irritation and roughening can occur if forearm muscles are required to do more than they are able to manage.

Two motions in particular are responsible for delivering punishment to the tendon: repeated tight gripping while turning the palm upward (supination) or tight gripping while turning the palm downward (pronation). These motions occur often while you garden, with or without a tool in your hand.

Just think about it: When you're yanking out weeds, for instance, you repetitively make a tight, clenching motion with the palm of your hand held in a downward position. After a period of time, fatigue is bound to occur, even for someone with considerable arm strength. But for the person whose arms are weak, pain or, even worse, injury can result. That's exactly why it's not only important to strengthen your arms for the tasks you tackle, but equally important to know when to stop working at an activity, such as weeding, to give your arms a well-deserved rest.

Chores that involve lugging (tools) and tugging (the hose) require arm power that can be improved by working with handheld weights. Even light ones (three to five pounds) are effective for building and maintaining your arms' capacity to manage tasks more comfortably.

When exercising your arms, with or without weights, move slowly and carefully. Moving your arms too quickly, particularly when using weights, can cause strains and tears in the arm muscles. The same applies while you work at your chores, whether that's pulling at resistant weeds or lifting a heavy rock.

The exercises I've included in this section of the book focus on stretching and strengthening the arms, both with and without weights. Because of the nature of the movements, your shoulders will also derive a benefit, a good thing because many gardening tasks, such as digging, weeding, and winding in the hose, not only require arm strength but shoulder power, too.

If you have never worked with handheld weights, start light; even working with a one-pound weight in each hand will eventually have a strengthening effect. And, please take note: if you suffer from arthritic hands, you want to be particularly careful not to take on more weight than you can comfortably handle.

ARM STRENGTHENERS

#1 Wall Push-Up
Position: Stand facing a wall at arm's length, feet comfortably apart and parallel. Place your palms on the wall with your fingers up. Keep your shoulder blades down and your abdominal muscles pulled in.

Movement: Slowly bend your elbows while taking four counts to lean into the wall. (Your elbows should bend down toward the floor.) Only go in as far as your arms can control the weight of your body. Then take four counts to push your body back away from the wall. Make sure to keep leaning your weight forward onto your hands when you begin straightening your arms; otherwise, you will use momentum to come away from the wall instead of arm strength. Repeat twelve times.

Note: If this seems too easy, slow down the count and take six or eight counts to move in and out. As you move toward and away from the wall, you should feel a mild stretching in your calf muscles.

You can also do this exercise in a slightly different way to specifically improve the strength of your *weaker* arm. Follow the instructions for the two-arm exercise except put your stronger arm down at your side and center your weaker arm on the wall between the spots where you placed both of your palms.

Slowly bend your elbow (point it diagonally down toward the floor) and lean toward the wall, again taking the four counts. Then slowly push back away from the wall by straightening your elbow. Just be sure not to lock it when you finish extending your arm. An even more challenging way to do this one-arm push-up is by placing your arm directly in front of your shoulder instead of centering it in front of your chest.

#2 Push-Up

Position: Kneel on all fours with your arms straight down from your shoulders; do not lock your elbows. Open your fingers slightly, pressing them down firmly and point them forward or slightly out. Extend your feet so the tops are on the floor. Make sure they reach straight back; do not let them turn in or out. (This foot position ensures knee comfort and protection.) Now walk your hands forward approximately ten inches. This change in your "all fours" placement will take your thighs out of the perpendicular and move them into a slight forward diagonal line.

Movement: Slowly, in four counts, bend your elbows and lower your body as you inhale. Then take four counts to lift your body by slowly straightening your arms as you exhale. Repeat six times.

#3 Arm Lift

Position: Stand with your feet comfortably apart and parallel, knees slightly bent. Hold a weight in each hand, palms in, arms straight down at your sides.

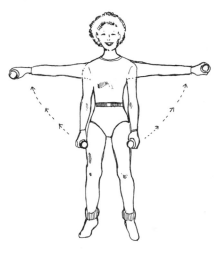

Movement: Lift the weights up to shoulder level before lowering them to the starting position. Use the same path for the up-and-down motion. Exhale up, inhale down. Repeat twelve times. Then repeat twelve times lifting the weights in front of your body to chest level.

"There is nothing like gardening to keep one young; it is everywhere concerned with life, and who can grow old in the presence of perpetual youth?"

H. H. THOMAS

#4 Curls

Position: Stand with your feet parallel and about sixteen inches apart,

▿▿▿▿▿ **TIP** ▿▿▿▿▿

After a bath or shower, massage a dab of nail conditioner into your nail beds. Look for products that contain natural emollients like sesame or avocado oil. Badger Healing Balm, available at garden supply stores, is a good choice. Legend says Paul Bunyon once said, "Give me enough Badger, and I can heal the cracks in the Grand Canyon." I don't know about that, but with ingredients such as olive oil, natural beeswax, castor oil, and aloe vera extract, it sure does wonders for hard-working hands.

knees slightly flexed. Hold a weight in each hand at arm's length at your sides, palms facing up.

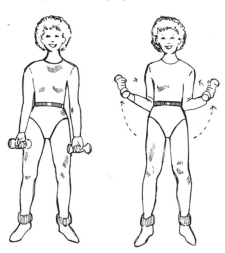

Movement: Curl your arms up bringing the weights to your shoulders, keeping your elbows close to your sides. Inhale up, exhale down.

Repeat twenty times. Then change position and rest your arms on your thighs in front of your body, palms facing up. Curl the weights up to shoulder level. Repeat twenty times. You can also do the curls alternating arms.

Note: To prevent your neck muscles from tensing, which can happen if you keep your head in a fixed position for too long while using weights, from time to time move your head slowly from right to left.

#5 Arm Push

Position: Lie on your back with your knees bent, feet apart and parallel. Hold a weight in each hand, palms facing forward, elbows bent and resting on the floor at shoulder level.

Movement: Keeping your abdominal muscles pulled in and your back flat, take two counts to push the weights up until your arms are almost straight (do not lock your elbows). Then lower the weights in two counts. Repeat twenty times. Exhale up, inhale down. Then repeat twenty times with the palms facing in.

DAMAGE CONTROL: GARDEN ELBOW AND GARDEN ARM

When I talk of garden elbow, I speak from experience, having endured such a bad case that by the end of summer, I was unable to dead-head a daisy without distress. This condition generally results from overworking (something common among weekend gardeners), which then leads to fatigue in the arm. Armed (no pun intended) with an arsenal of tools, but not an abundance of time, we try to accomplish the impossible in a mere two days.

Although overuse is the prime cause of tendinitis in most cases, it can also occur if you garden with too much enthusiasm early in the season

▽ ▽ ▽ ▽ ▽ **TIP** ▽ ▽ ▽ ▽ ▽

To keep soil from getting under your fingernails, moisten a bar of soap before gardening and run your nails along it so that the soap cakes under them forming a protective layer.

when your arms are simply not ready for strenuous work. So if you haven't exercised your arms all winter, aside from knitting or moving chess pieces by the fireplace, and you attack your gardening chores with utter abandon in the spring, you could end up with a case of garden elbow.

Soreness occurs in the elbow joint's tendons and ligaments as well as lower in the forearm. In fact, sufferers do not experience pain inside their elbow; they feel it instead on the outside of the joint just above the elbow crease, which was exactly what I experienced.

Pain is felt in this particular spot because it's the point at which the major muscles in the forearm are anchored to the upper-arm bone by a tendon, the point where irritation and roughening can occur if forearm muscles are asked to do more than they are comfortable doing. You feel the discomfort not only on the site of injury, but above and below it as well. In fact, when the condition is really severe, tingling can occur, which it did in my case, all the way down the forearm and into the fingers. The repetitive, gripping motions (i.e. weeding) that gardening involves, with or without tools, can be the cause of this uncomfortable, bothersome condition.

Garden elbow is not the only discomfort that can result from working with too much enthusiasm and intensity; there's also garden arm. Here the pain is really in the muscles of the forearm rather than at their attachment points at the elbow, or at the muscle-tendon junction.

However, it's not necessary to retire your hoe and head for the hammock if you are bothered by arm and elbow discomfort, not if you tend to it early. Because I was unnecessarily stoic (translation: stubborn), I allowed my condition to worsen by continuing to garden despite the pain. But I don't recommend this course of action. (Do as I say, not as I do!) Although the pain may be mild, take care of it. You will be able to take care of your garden then, too.

Ice and nonprescription anti-inflammatory medications can help relieve the discomfort; however, rest must also be part of the treatment. You can't garden "through it" and expect the condition to improve. You don't have to throw in the trowel for the season, but you really should refrain from using the sore arm long enough to allow the inflammation to subside, after which time you should begin a forearm strengthening program. But unless you give the arm adequate rest and wait until the symptoms have significantly improved, you may very well have to throw in the trowel for the remainder of the season, as well as all your other tools.

Ice is generally the preferred treatment for tendinitis, although heat is useful in the later stages. So aside from giving the elbow or arm some rest, you want to apply ice to the painful area several times a day for about fifteen or twenty minutes at a time. To protect your skin, place a towel or washcloth between the pack and the area you're icing. I find the paper cup ice application (see page 14) works particularly well for treating arm strain, particularly elbow soreness.

Also available are straps and lightweight braces that you can wear while you garden, providing you don't have a severe case of tendinitis, in which case you really should not be gardening at all. Not only will a strap help reduce stress to the tendon, but it also gives external support to the affected area. One word of caution, however, about wearing an arm brace or strap while you garden: make sure it's not too tight; otherwise, it could compromise your circulation.

If the tendinitis is not addressed early and appropriately, it can and often does become chronic, a condition you want to avoid. When temporary rest, ice, and over-the-counter anti-inflammatory medication do not reduce or eliminate the problem, other treatments to consider are acupuncture, massage, or physical therapy. If the symptoms remain severe after trying the above-mentioned approaches, an injection of cortisone might be necessary. But again, I repeat, if you're wise, you will try to arrest the tendinitis before it becomes severe by first resting the arm and then by strengthening it.

Take my word for it. If you wait two or three months before seeing a doctor or physical therapist, without relief from home treatment, you might, as I did, find your symptoms especially tough to shake.

Although you might have to temporarily refrain (not retire) from gardening, rest alone is not the only answer. Studies have shown that weak forearm muscles increase your chance for elbow tendinitis in the first place. So if your pain is beginning to significantly subside, you could benefit from the following exercises that gently but effectively strengthen the muscles that need conditioning. But even before attempting these, give your arm a few days of rest. Find a comfortable spot under a shade tree and instead of weeding, do some reading.

The first exercise I'm suggesting strengthens the forearm. To do this, grip a two- or three-pound weight with the hand of the sore arm. Place your forearm, palm down, on a desk or tabletop with your wrist at the edge of the support, elbow bent.

Slowly rotate the forearm clockwise 180 degrees, turning your palm upward. The movement should take five seconds. Return to starting position and relax for two seconds. In time, you want to build up to twelve repetitions comfortably.

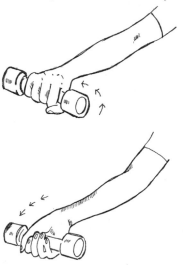

The second exercise strengthens your wrist flexors and is also done with a two- or three-pound weight. Again, place your arm, this time palm up, on a support as you did for the first exercise. Bend your wrist upward toward the ceiling as far as you can and hold for five seconds. Return to the starting position and relax for three seconds. Gradually increase to twelve repetitions.

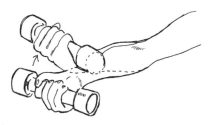

In my particular case, massage was extremely effective for relieving the discomfort of tendinitis. I worked with a physical therapist who combined trigger point massage with heat treatments and electrical stimulation (pulses designed to mimic normal muscle contractions) twice a week for nearly four weeks, which is just how long it took before my arm was completely healed.

Having had that experience, I made it a point to find tools that would reduce, or better yet eliminate, stress on my arm. One tool I particularly like is a gooseneck hoe featured in Walt Nicke's Garden Talk catalog. Not only is it light and strong, but superbly balanced as well. According to the company, "No weed can hide from it." And they're right. It reaches in to cultivate tight spots so my arm doesn't have to overwork.

At Ward's Nursery in Great Barrington, Massachusetts, one of my favorite sources for plant matter and equipment, not to mention horticultural advice, I came upon a unique and handy tool, the Soil Scoop. This lightweight hand tool has a rounded body ending in a pointed tip and serrated edges, not unlike a pregnant grapefruit spoon. It's appealing because it has dual horticultural uses: turned one way, it can dig or cultivate; turned the other, it can hold soil like a shovel or trowel. Best of all, it's really comfortable to handle. You can order a Soil Scoop from W. Atlee Burpee and Company.

▼

"At a passing glance from a distance you don't see anything of the gardener but his rump; everything else, like his head, arms, and legs, is hidden underneath."

KAREL ČAPEK

Your Hands and Fingers

Your two miracle workers are certainly put to the test while you work in the garden. Yanking away at vines, digging holes for hundreds of bulbs, or even light work such as deadheading flowers or sowing seeds requires hand strength and dexterity.

The joints and the twenty-seven bones (lots of bones for a little area) in your hands give them the mobility needed for seeding, weeding, digging, and an array of other jobs. In addition, your hands have many muscles that allow you to move your hand bones in a wide variety of ways. But hand muscles need to be more than just powerful; they need to be able to stretch to carry out chores comfortably—and many actually do involve carrying.

Gardeners who regularly use their hands for other activities such as typing, knitting, or playing the piano are more apt to have agile, limber fingers. In fact, challenging your hand and finger muscles and joints on a daily basis does pay off in

the garden, unless, of course, you overwork your hands, which can result in carpal tunnel syndrome (see page 28).

Needless to say, arthritis of the fingers makes some tasks (weeding, for instance) more difficult to manage. If your fingers are arthritic, you should avoid getting into certain positions, such as supporting yourself on your hands and knees while you crawl on all fours. This position places far too much stress on vulnerable finger joints.

By no means, however, should arthritis keep you from gardening. In fact, if you do suffer from arthritic fingers, it's very important that you continue to use your finger joints; otherwise, they stiffen more. The key is not to overuse them.

▼

"There is nothing pleasanter than spading when the ground is soft and damp."

JOHN STEINBECK

So what's the best way to keep your hands in shape for gardening? By maintaining hand strength and agility as best you can. To a great extent, this can be achieved by practicing basic hand strengthening exercises such as the ones I'm recommending. These easy-to-do movements are specifically designed to keep your hands strong and your fingers nimble.

HAND STRENGTHENERS

#1 Ball Squeeze

Position: Hold a semisoft rubber ball (about two and a half inches in diameter) in your hand. You can do this while standing or seated. In fact, if you carry a ball with you during the day (keep one in your purse or attaché case), this exercise can be done whenever you have a minute to spare.

Movement: First, squeeze the ball in one hand with all your fingers and your thumb. Maintain the squeeze until you feel your hand tire somewhat. Then let it relax. Repeat six times. Then repeat with your other hand. Another way to exercise with the ball is to use one finger and thumb. Start by squeezing the ball between your little finger and thumb, then your ring finger and thumb, middle finger and thumb, and finally index finger and thumb. Do six squeezes with each finger. To stretch and relax your hands after squeezing the ball, just shake them out.

Note: Always exercise both hands. In fact, do extra repetitions with your nonwriting hand. This will develop strength and dexterity in your other hand so that it can take over when your "favorite" tires.

#2 Hand Stretch

Position: Extend your hands in front of you with your fingers close together.

Movement: Separate the fingers until a stretching tension is felt. Hold for eight seconds, then relax. Repeat ten times.

Note: You can also do this with a rubber band around the fingers to create more resistance when you stretch the fingers apart.

#3 Finger Bend

Position: Extend your hands in front of you, fingers slightly apart.

Movement: Bend the fingers at the knuckles and squeeze for ten seconds. Relax and repeat ten times.

#4 Wrist Mobilizer

Position: Stretch your arms out in front of you at shoulder level, palms down.

Movement: Flex your hands upward strongly, feeling the stretch under your arms. Hold for six counts, then drop your hands from the wrists and hold for six counts. Repeat six times.

▼

"Green fingers are the extensions of a verdant heart."

RUSSELL PAGE

DAMAGE CONTROL: CARPAL TUNNEL SYNDROME AND FINGERNAIL FUNGUS

I'm convinced that besides sniffing each other out, gardeners can spot one another simply by doing a "hand check" anytime from early spring to late fall. Show me a woman in midsummer whose nails are superbly manicured and you can bet she's spending her time reading, not weeding.

Although gardening may seem a genteel pastime to those who have never taken a trowel in hand, those of us who crawl around on our hands and knees know the down and dirty truth. The sport of gardening can leave its mark: chapped and cracked skin, broken nails, cuts and scratches, fungal infections, blisters, and splinters.

Hands down, there's one way to avoid a continual collision with Mother Nature: Wear gloves while you garden. They prevent blisters when raking, digging, or pruning, and they also prevent you from having hand combat with a camouflaged snake, slug, or a moribund mini-animal that has chosen to turn into compost in your prized perennial bed.

As for your choice of gloves, buy smart not cheap. Protection is the key, and inexpensive gloves are usually poorly made and become tattered and torn quickly. Over the years, I've purchased high quality, durable gloves through Walt Nicke's Garden Talk catalog, one of my favorite mail-order suppliers for great garden tools and associated matter. One pair of gloves I'm partial to is the Women's Work Glove, specifically designed to fit the contours of women's hands. These durable gloves are made of sturdy but flexible unlined pigskin suede. They really do, as promised, remain supple even after being wet—meaning they also launder well.

The other gloves that have lasted for years are the sheepskin garden gloves, also from the same catalog. These are reinforced in the palm, thumb, and forefinger with double thickness leather, yet they mold beautifully to the hand. According to the catalog, "They're so supple you don't even have to remove them to write on your garden labels." And they happen to be right.

My friend Robin who has an utterly glorious, overgrown garden in Lyme, Connecticut, bought me a pair of Wonder Gloves for Valentine's Day, a loving gift for my hands. And the name is not deceptive: these orange hand savers (sold at garden supply stores) really work wonders, particularly for muddy, wet jobs. Not only are they incredibly durable (I'm a menace with gloves), but they're truly waterproof as well. But what sets them apart is the fit; you can actually pick up a seed with them on.

For many years, before I discovered Wonder Gloves, I wore lined, rubber kitchen gloves for wet gardening chores. But Wonder Gloves are far more flexible; they're made with a vinyl shell covering a seamless cotton liner that protects and insulates the hands. Available in sizes ranging from petite to extra large, they're must-have gloves for wet work.

In fact, if you want even more protection, you can purchase them, as I do, in one size larger than you would ordinarily wear. This allows extra room for a thin cotton liner (While*U*Sleep Gloves) to be worn inside the Wonder Glove. Not only does the liner offer added protection, but it absorbs perspiration as well. While*U*Sleep Gloves, or similar cotton liners, are sold at pharmacies.

In addition to the lesser afflictions, there is one hand problem to really avoid: carpal tunnel syndrome. Again, I speak from experience. Nip it in the bud! As more and more men and women discover the glories of gardening, CTS afflicts an ever-growing number, especially those who try to maniacally cram all their gardening into a mere two days. The weekend gardener is, indeed, a prime candidate for CTS.

What is CTS exactly, and how do you keep it at arm's length? The term is actually appropriate because the carpal tunnel is formed by the wrist bones (known as the carpals) and the transverse ligament. The carpal bones are held in place by this ligament that runs across the base of the palm, not unlike the strap of a watch. Through this short tunnel pass the tendons that travel down the wrist and move the fingers.

The median nerve, which supplies the muscles that allow you to move your thumb and make a fist around a tool handle, also shares space in this cramped passageway. If your finger-operating tendons become irritated because of overuse (tightly gripping a tool for too long), they may swell and press on this nerve.

The symptoms of such compression may be slight at first, typically numbness, pain, weakness, and a tingling or pins-and-needles sensation in the thumb, index finger, and middle finger. If untreated, the pain can radiate to the elbow, upper arm, and shoulder.

Eventually, the nerve impulses in the wrist may be short-circuited, causing nerves in the thumb, index finger, and middle finger to "starve" and the thumb muscles to progressively waste away—a strong enough reason for not wanting this problem to become acute. Once recognized, the symptoms should be treated early before lasting damage occurs.

For me, discomfort often worsened at night, when I was awakened by a tingling or numbness. Several of my gardening pals (generally women) related similar nighttime symptoms. (Combine the tingles with hot flashes and you can forget about getting any sleep!) The tingling is often due to the positions the wrist gets placed in during sleep. For instance, if you sleep on your stomach with your arms and wrists bent and flexed under you, continuous pressure is being placed on your wrists. Naturally, this will further exacerbate the problem. To relieve nighttime tingling and numbness, shake out the hand or hang it over the edge of the bed.

One approach to healing the hand is to immobilize the wrist, which is exactly what I did. A static wrist splint allows the fingers to wiggle freely while keeping the wrist in a neutral position so that it has a chance to heal. Wearing a splint is generally the first line of treatment. In fact, I wore a splint at night as well to prevent my hand from drifting into positions that would press on the nerve. I was able to garden while I wore the splint, although my projects were somewhat curtailed. (Stuffing a splintered hand into a glove, even if it's a Wonder Glove, isn't so easy.)

Because you may have to wear the splint for three or four weeks, which is what I ended up doing, proper fit is very important. If the splint is too tight, it may cause more swelling and aggravate the problem. If on the other hand (no pun intended), the splint is too loose, it won't provide any protection. And that's exactly why many therapists recommend a custom-made splint.

If you suffer from symptoms of CTS, do not ignore them. Seek the help of a professional, which in my case was an osteopath whom I deeply trust. Not only did he recommend that I wear the splint, but he also recommended a nonsteroidal anti-inflammatory drug (Advil). Included as well in my therapy was massage that targeted my wrist and fingers.

Fortunately for me, my hand repaired before I had to consider treating it more aggressively, with a cortisone injection or, still worse, with surgery, the treatment often suggested for severe cases that do not respond to other therapies. I strongly urge you to nip CTS in the bud.

Speaking of nipping and snipping, that's just why so many gardeners end up with CTS in the first place. Repetitive manual tasks, particularly those requiring wrist movement, can cause inflammation and swelling to even the hardiest hands. So garden smart: use your head as well as your hands.

Even if you're in the midst of an important task that demands completion, at the first sign of hand discomfort, stop what you're doing, take off your gloves, and gently shake out your hands. This relaxes the hand muscles and encourages circulation. In fact, numerous other safe and simple exercises that relieve hand strain and fatigue can be done right in the garden. They are included in chapter 2.

As I mentioned previously, do not maniacally attack your chores in the spring; gradually increase the duration of your work so that your hands have a chance to get accustomed to the demands and positions required in the months to come. To keep your hands from becoming overly fatigued, make it a point to alternate strenuous tasks with lighter work.

Also, work on developing ambidexterity, a sure survival tactic for your hands. For chores like weeding, challenge the other hand to avoid overuse. Try as well to avoid keeping your hand in a fixed position for too long; just moving it slightly makes a difference.

Speaking of positions, I'm often guilty of doing this myself: avoid leaning on the heel of your hands (wrists hyperextended), with your body weight pushed forward and arms rigid, while you crawl around the garden on all fours. It's just too much weight (even if you are a lightweight) for your wrists to assume.

Now, I'm not saying that you should avoid crawling on all fours, not at all, but you should not remain on your hands and knees for too long. As soon as your wrists or hands begin to ache at all, take the weight (meaning you) off them.

Of course, the tools you use will also make a huge difference in terms of hand health and comfort. They should be in good working order so that your hands do not have to work harder than necessary. That means keep them sharp and oiled. It also might mean getting rid of any that do not work well for you, no matter how much you paid for them. Look for lightweight tools with comfortable grips that allow you to work while keeping your wrist in as neutral a position as possible.

And remember, too, tools should fit your body size. My guess is that even way back then in that original garden, Adam and Eve did not share the same tools. What was right for him most likely did not work for her. Generally, smaller body types need tools with adjustable handles or smaller grips. Tools designed especially for women and senior gardeners (Garden Gals) are offered, for instance, in the One to Grow On catalog. They're perfect for small hands and gardeners with lessened hand strength.

One tool that I really love because it molds into the palm of my hand and allows me to dig and weed with no wrist twisting whatsoever is the Clawdia, a palm-fitting cultivator that I purchased through Devon Lake Enterprises. This lightweight, small, black-and-red tool rests in the palm of the hand, with the fingers outstretched along the tines or curved over the grip between the tines. Named after the inventor, the Clawdia has proven to be the perfect little gift for friends who garden, particularly my more "mature" pals who suffer from arthritic fingers. Wrapped in pretty floral paper, with a sprig of lavender tucked under the ribbon, it's the ideal present for the gardener who has everything, including aching hands.

Two other tools, both of which I purchased through catalogs, have made gardening easier on my hands. One is the ARS Super Light Aluminum Shear (purchased from A. M. Leonard), which boasts unique ergonomic design features. These shears are truly powerful yet featherweight and require a minimum of hand strength, which is a real plus, particularly if you suffer from arthritis.

The other tool I wouldn't be without is appropriately called the Ideal Weeder, available through Walt Nicke's Garden Talk catalog. This particular weeder has a 3/4-inch-wide blade that is well sharpened on all of its edges, including the tip, which I successfully use to pick out small weeds in close spaces.

In addition to actual tools that keep your hands from overworking,

there are handles (straight and D-grips) that can be repositioned at any point along a tool's shaft so that a rake or hoe can become more ergonomically appropriate for you. Most garden supply stores carry these tool appendages, or they can be purchased through catalogs, as can grips that slide onto your tool handles for a more comfortable, nonslip hold. One to Grow On, a good source for ergonomic garden tools and accessories, offers a variety of these appendages.

Because tools are so crucial and hand care and health are so important for comfortable gardening, I've listed (at the back of the book) several of my favorite mail-order suppliers that carry ergonomic gardening tools. If, however, you order a tool by mail and discover, as I have on more than one occasion, that it's not right for you, you can return it for a refund or replacement (before of course you plunge it into the soil).

"Soon her fingers were deftly pulling out tufts of grass and violets from around the bleeding heart; nothing like weeding to unknot the mind."

MAY SARTON

If you are resistant to wearing gloves because you love the feel of the good earth between your hands, there's a good chance you could end up with a case of fingernail fungus.

Anyone who gardens is apt to suffer from scrapes and bruises of the skin around the nails, which is not so serious. What is serious, however, is when these scrapes and scratches allow access to bacteria and the yeast fungus *Candida albicans*. These are the major causes of *paronychia*, or infection of the skin around the nail, which is not a pretty sight. And, again, speaking from personal experience, I can add it doesn't feel so good either.

For starters, do not attempt, as I did, to self-diagnose the specie of fungal infection you have. There are various types and the "one size fits all approach" will not work. Also, do not soak your fungus with the hope that this will make it better; fungus hangs out in moisture. Don't make it easier to survive by giving it a nice, warm bath. You will only make it worse. Remember, too, once fungus finds a fingerhold, it can spread from nail to nail.

So how do you get rid of a fungal infection? It's really not so easy, particularly if, like me, you're unwilling to take oral medication due to their side effects. The first step is determining just what kind of infection you have; and that's not for you to determine (unless of course you're a dermatologist, in which case you probably wouldn't have a fungus in the first place). Let a doctor take a

look, and not just any doctor; seek the advice of a dermatologist or a physician who specializes in nails, which is what I did, although, as usual, I waited too long.

Usually doctors rely on two conventional diagnostic tests: microscopic examination of scrapings taken from under the nail and/or test-tube cultures of these scrapings. However, neither is 100 percent accurate. According to my dermatologist, known in New York City gardening circles as the nail guru, about 30 percent of these test results suggest no infection, when in fact there is one. For best results, samples, according to him, should always be sent to labs that specialize in nail fungus.

Because fungus cultures may take as much as six weeks to grow, treatment often proceeds before test results are in. In those cases, most doctors will begin with conservative measures, trimming back the infected nail and prescribing a topical antifungal cream or liquid. Unfortunately, the topical ointments and antifungal lotions often will not cure severe fungal infections. Since the fungus has penetrated the nail and its bed, effective medication must do the task.

That's where the oral antifungal drugs come in. These medications enter the nail matrix, the white half-moon from which a nail grows. As new nail grows, the saturated cells form an antifungal barrier. Many of the new drugs that are used currently act quicker by penetrating directly into the nail from the nail bed. In fact, several new drugs, currently awaiting FDA approval, show promise in shortening treatments, minimizing side effects, and preventing recurrences.

HANDY TIPS FOR HEALTHY NAILS

▶ The longer your nails, the more room for dirt to get under them. Keep them clipped or filed back so that they do not extend beyond the tips of the fingers.

▶ Sterilize clippers used on infected nails to avoid spreading a fungus to the healthy nails.

▶ Do not let your cuticles get so dry they crack, leaving openings for infection. Keep cuticles moisturized with petroleum jelly or cuticle cream, which should be applied before you head for the garden as well as after you clean up.

▶ Refrain from cutting your cuticles. The cuticle (living tissue) is a seal-ant that protects the nail matrix; disturbing this seal increases your risk of developing infections.

▶ Wash your gardening gloves frequently to keep dirt particles out. Machine washing in hot or cold soapy water kills the nail fungus in fabric.

▶ If you are prone to fungus infections, apply diluted tea tree oil to the nail and cuticle; it's an antifungal weapon of the first order. Or ask your doctor to prescribe a topical antifungal ointment or gel. Apply it daily before you garden as *preventive medicine*, not unlike sunscreen.

▶ Hands burn, too, so apply sunscreen to the top of your hands, even if you do stuff them into gloves most of the time. Sunright 23 for Face and Hands by Nu Skin is a good choice. Or, in lieu of a sunscreen, apply a moisturizer that contains sunscreen such as Daily UV Protectant Beauty Fluid by Oil of Olay (SPF 15).

Your Knees

Stress on your knees while you garden comes from all directions: front, back, and both sides. When you're squatting to pick up your tools or pushing the cart uphill, your knees are being constantly called on (not to mention crawled on).

Granted, it's no fun to garden when your knees are unhappy and constantly letting you know it. And they will protest if they're not properly protected, which means more than simply wearing knee pads or using a kneeling stool while you work. Knee protection comes not only from strengthening the appropriate muscles but from moving the correct way.

Take squatting: unless it's done properly you can really stress your knees by straining or even tearing ligaments, so you want to do it the right way or not at all. Because I'm quite agile by nature, along with having studied yoga (a sure flexibility enhancer) for many years, sitting on my heels while I work is comfortable: in fact it's a position I favor.

To squat the correct way, you really should keep your heels flat, otherwise, far too much pressure is placed on your knees. If you squat with your heels off the ground (a position I often observe gardeners in), you can very possibly damage your knee ligaments. Avoid a deep squatting position with your weight forward on your toes, instead of on your entire foot.

Put another way, if you cannot manage a low squat with your heels planted flat on the ground, you should refrain from squatting. And yes, it is difficult to do a proper squat (common in Near East and Far East Asian countries) if your calf muscles and Achilles tendons (which attach your calf muscles to the back of your heel bone) are not adequately stretched and flexible.

On the other hand, when you do squat the proper, safe way (heels flat), you support your body weight on the bones of your feet (horizontally placed) and on the bones of your legs (vertically positioned), instead of on your vulnerable knee ligaments and cartilages, with the bones of your legs precariously balanced on a diagonal.

If you do work on your knees, whether remaining in place or crawling around on all fours, it's important as well to avoid staying on your knees too long. To take the pressure and weight off them, stand up from time to time.

Extra cushioning and support can also come from wearing knee pads or kneeling on a cushion while you work, particularly when the ground is cold or damp. This is especially important if you suffer from arthritic knees. You might want to purchase a kneeling stool, such as the one manufactured by Step 2, available at garden centers and hardware stores that feature gardening equipment. Not only is this particular model less costly than many of the kneeling stools imported from England, but it's far lighter and thus easier to carry.

▼

The weird and wacky positions you get into while you garden will obviously affect the condition of your knees at the end of a day. Protecting them involves learning how to move correctly when you bend or crawl on them, as well as strengthening the quadriceps, which, when conditioned and strong, give your knees the support they deserve.

You have to strengthen the quads the right way, but that does not mean by practicing deep knee bends. Although knee bends are intended to strengthen all the leg muscles, particularly the big quadriceps in the front of the thighs, done in the traditional way, they are among the most harmful exercises. The problem occurs when the bend is too deep and goes beyond the place where the thigh muscles hold and control your body weight.

So what is the best way to practice a knee bend to strengthen your thighs? Slow, controlled, and not too deep. Try it this way: Stand tall with your feet about shoulder-width apart and parallel. Slowly bend at the knees until your thighs and calves

---
▽

"Adam was a gardener, and God who made him sees. That half a proper gardener's work is done upon his knees."
RUDYARD KIPLING

△
---

form approximately a ninety degree angle. Hold the position for six slow counts before you lift to the starting position. Your arms should be extended in front at chest level for balance, with your palms facing down.

Whenever you practice any knee-bending movement, you want to make certain to keep your back straight and your head erect because a forward lean can strain your back. In addition, it's very important, for the sake of your knees, that you bend them with control, meaning not too quickly.

If you find the knee-bending exercise difficult to do without a support, stand with your hands resting on a kitchen counter, desk, or any waist high piece of furniture. Then, as you get stronger, you can use your hands less until you're finally able to manage the exercise without holding on at all. The following two exercises effectively and safely strengthen the quadriceps.

KNEE STRENGTHENERS

#1 Quadriceps Strengthener
Position: Stand near a wall or hold a support for balance. Your supporting

---

▽ ▽ ▽ ▽ ▽ **TIP** ▽ ▽ ▽ ▽ ▽

What does your skin have in common with a soft-boiled egg? Both may be overcooked within a few minutes.

leg should be relaxed (do not lock the knee) and the foot pointed straight ahead. Bend the other knee so that the lower leg is almost at a right angle to its own thigh.

Movement: Slowly straighten the leg by extending the lower leg without lowering the knee. The foot should be flexed. In this raised position, pulse the leg upward six times, then bend it to the original position. Repeat the sequence four times. Then repeat on the other leg.

Note: Take care to hold your upper body in a vertical line and your abdominal muscles in.

#2 Forward Lunge

Position: Stand with one foot well ahead of the other (about ten to fourteen inches apart). Relax your arms at your sides.

Movement: Slowly take six counts to bend both knees; lower your body while keeping your upper body in an almost upright vertical position. Feel your body weight over your front thigh. The heel of your back foot lifts up while the heel of the

▼

front foot remains flat throughout the exercise. When the knee of your back leg is almost on the ground, take six counts to straighten your legs, raising your body up again. The front foot and leg should be positioned so that at the lowest point, your thigh and lower leg are at a right angle. Repeat four times, then place the back leg forward to repeat on the other leg.

Note: This movement is more difficult than the previous exercise since it requires greater balance. Make sure that you do not feel any discomfort in your knees. If you do feel knee strain, adjust the space between your legs, forward or back, and do not lower your body down quite so far.

▼

"Spring flowers are long since gone. Summer's bloom hangs limp on every terrace. The gardener's feet drag a bit on the dusty path and the hinge in his back is full of creaks."
LOUISE SEYMOUR JONES

DAMAGE CONTROL: STIFFNESS AND ARTHRITIS

Because gardening involves so much getting up and down from the ground (unless of course you cultivate raised beds only), by the end of the day, even strong knees know they've had a workout. If your knees are even the least bit arthritic, all that bending and crawling around can leave them feeling quite uncomfortable.

Knee discomfort, however, can be reduced significantly if the muscles that surround the knee are properly warmed up and stretched before you head for the garden. Two simple movements that reduce stiffness and enhance knee mobility can be done right in your bedroom in the morning, the first before you even leave your bed.

For this exercise, lie on your back with one knee drawn to your chest and your hands clasped around the lower leg, just beneath the knee. The other leg should hang free with the knee just slightly over the edge of the bed. You want to hold this position, allowing the hanging leg to stretch out for at least 30 seconds before repeating the stretch with the other leg.

After you've completed the bed stretch, stand up and hold on to a dresser or a heavy table for balance. Take hold of your foot near the ankle and gently ease your heel up toward your buttock without placing too much pressure on the foot. Hold the stretch for about 10 seconds, then lower the leg and repeat on the other side. (This is what joggers do to stretch their quads.) And that's all there is to this simple two-part morning knee-stretching routine.

You will add to your knees' capacity to resist injury while you garden not only by conditioning your quadriceps, but also by stretching and strengthening the hamstrings. So here's an easy exercise specifically for that purpose: Lie on the floor with your knees bent. Extend one leg up and hook the foot onto a long scarf or belt that you can hold at each end. Straighten out the leg as much as possible without straining and gently tug on the ends of the scarf until you feel a gentle pull behind the upper thigh. Hold the stretch. When the muscles relax somewhat, tug on the scarf a bit more. Then switch to the other leg.

If you do garden into and beyond your "goldenrod" years, it's quite possible that you will develop some arthritis in your knees; in fact, it's only natural. Not only is this condition common, it has a long and well-documented lineage among living creatures, dating back to cavemen and cavewomen. That's right. Even our prehistoric, horticulturally in-clined ancestors showed signs of osteoarthritic changes. Then and now, the signs are similar: a basic defense mechanism in the joints orders up the growth of new bone in the face of trauma, fractures, or the erosion of the smooth cartilage that lines the interior of joints.

So what do you do when a flare-up occurs? Should you continue gardening or head for the hammock or house? Pain tends to inhibit movement, which can be damaging with arthritis since you really should keep moving for the sake of your joints. Thirty percent of the knee joint's stability is maintained by the quadriceps and hamstrings, the muscles in the front and back of your thighs. If your knees hurt and you refrain from gardening (or any activity for that matter), these vital support muscles can waste away, which is just what you don't want to happen. "Use it or loose it," as the saying goes.

But obviously, you don't want to exacerbate the arthritis. It's unlikely, however, that moderate gardening will make your osteoarthritis worse. In fact, in the long run, it's extremely important to keep moving and to maintain strong, supple leg muscles, especially those serving the knees. Most physicians agree that resting the joint temporarily as well as taking aspirin or some other nonsteroidal anti-inflammatory medication can be very helpful when an arthritic flare-up erupts.

As you may know all too well, arthritic pain and stiffness, are usually worse in the morning, which means planning your garden chores for too early in the day might not be a good idea. Instead, plan to "dig in" a bit latter in the morning to give your knee joints adequate time to not only wake up but to loosen up. In fact, gardening, like other physical activities, is best done at a time in the day when you consistently feel in top form. Are you a morning glory or an evening primrose?

There are other sensible ways to keep your knees happy and healthy while you garden, whether you suffer from arthritis or not. If possible, try to divide your gardening into sensible, sane segments over the course of the week, just as you would any other workout. If you have a weekend property and have only two days to garden, at least try to spread the workload over the two-day period.

And if you're like me and lose all track of time once you're in the garden, bring a timer along. That's right. A timer can remind you to stop working and give your knees (and the rest of you) a time-out. I recommend a timer because if you get carried away (a common trait among gardeners), you probably forget to even check your watch. That's exactly why I use a timer; like the corset and wrist strap that I occasionally wear, a timer also puts the brakes on lunatic behavior.

Also for the sake of your knees, avoid any sharp, quick twisting or turning motions, which can stress the knee joints. For instance, when you're using a spade or shovel to dig soil to place elsewhere, if the elsewhere is to your right or to your left side, turn with your entire body, keeping your knees bent and relaxed. Never twist or swivel sharply with your knees locked or rigid. This stresses not only the knees, but your back as well.

Also be very careful of the positions you assume when working on the ground if you have any knee problems. For instance, sitting on your heels places far too much stress on the knees. Another position to avoid is sitting on the ground with your feet flared out to the sides since this can overstretch the inside ligaments of the knee. In fact, if your knees are at all vulnerable, you should avoid keeping them bent for any length of time, in any position, even while sitting on a stool to work. From time to time, get up and shake your legs to ease away the stiffness.

Another option to consider if your knees trouble you is raised beds. By cultivating raised beds, you will eliminate the need to constantly bend over to work at ground level. Also, working at a table instead of bending over when you're potting plants, for example, will lessen the stress and strain on your knees and your back.

Another knee-saving tactic is to use long-handled tools. Rakes, spades, and hoes can be purchased in lengths up to 6 feet. With the longer handles, you will be able to work on ground-level beds with more leverage and far less knee bending. Many of the tools offered in the A. M. Leonard catalog feature handles and heads that adjust for the size of the job and the size of the gardener. But a word of caution: generally, the longer the handle, the heavier the tool, and the more force it takes to both lift and use it.

Remember as well that joints pull together more tightly when they get cold, so it's important to keep your knees warm, particularly if they are arthritic and you garden in inclement weather. If you find that dampness and cold penetrate your jeans, overalls, or whatever you work in, you might want to wear nylon or cotton tights under your trousers for added warmth.

"Gardening is a matter of your enthusiasm holding up until your back gets used to it."

ANONYMOUS

Flexibility

Not only do you need strong, well-toned muscles for gardening, but they should also be elastic and flexible. Even something as simple as bending over to pick up your tools will be easier if your range of motion is not compromised by tight, taut muscles.

A flexible body is a more graceful body, which certainly has its advantages in the garden, where you have to get into all sorts of strange positions. Being awkward and klutzy can have you trampling instead of tiptoeing through the tulips, crushing everything underfoot. My point: A clumsy, inflexible gardener can create considerable wreckage.

I learned this very lesson by asking my husband Stephen (just once) to help me place a defiant soaker hose in the hilltop perennial bed. Understand, I love him dearly, but he's not exactly Fred Astaire when it comes to grace on his feet. In the process of helping me tame the resistant hose so that we could strategically place it throughout the bed, he managed to trample just about every dainty seedling. A more flexible, agile assistant might have done less damage.

In days of old, stretching exercises for flexibility enhancement generally consisted of fast bounces and jerky motions on the theory that the body's momentum would pull kinks out of tight muscles. That theory is about as sound as using human urine to deter the deer. (Stephen generously offered a sampling for our experiment.)

In fact, stretching in a forceful, bouncing manner can cause soreness and injury by tearing the cross fibers that hold your muscle fibers together. So forget about the "no pain, no gain" approach. It's all wrong. Stretching, when done correctly, should not be painful.

Correct stretching for flexibility enhancement requires that you hold the position (static stretch) until the tension in the muscle releases. This usually takes thirty seconds to one minute, so please do not rush through these stretches simply to get them done. In fact, it's better not to do them at all if you are going to

rush. If a stretch is done correctly, your muscle tension should diminish slightly within a few seconds; if it does not, or if the stretch becomes more painful while you hold it, ease up a bit.

Unlike strengthening exercises that call for numerous repetitions, with flexibility stretches, you want to practice the movement slowly, stretching for a comfortable duration, which at first might be as little as eight or ten seconds. Eventually, with practice, you will be able to extend the "holding pattern" for approximately thirty to sixty seconds.

If your body is not familiar with stretching, your natural response to the sensation might be one of tightening up, if only a little bit. So be aware that your body may respond in a way that can temporarily inhibit the stretch you set out to do. If you feel yourself tightening up, you need to command yourself by saying "let go" or "relax" or "stay loose," or whatever words evoke a relaxing response. Remember, too, not everyone can gain the same amount of flexibility. Although joints are fomed differently in each individual, everyone's ligaments can gain elasticity given time and patience.

When you practice any of the following five flexibility stretches, don't force yourself to hold the stretch any longer than is comfortable for you, even if I call for a one-minute duration. Take the signals from your own body. Try to move into the stretch until you reach the point where you feel a mild tension, which should subside as you hold the position.

If it does not ease up, or if you experience any pain, ease off slightly and find a degree of tension that is comfortable, yet challenging. Always stop at the point where you feel that the stretch has gone as far as it wants to for the present time.

While practicing the following flexibility enhancers, keep your breathing slow and fluid. When you hold the stretch, avoid holding your breath. If you find that a position inhibits your natural breathing pattern, then you're probably not relaxed and should ease up on the stretch somewhat. With time, you will no longer have to count the seconds for each stretch; instead, you will begin to hold the position simply by the way it feels.

If your flexibility is limited and it's difficult to reach, bend, or turn with ease in the garden, these five stretches should extend your range of motion, making your chores easier to manage. As I mentioned earlier, being more flexible and agile affects your coordination, too. Enhanced flexibility will allow you to move with greater freedom and better balance, whether you're working in an upright position or on the ground. And there's yet another important factor: stretched muscles resist stress far better than unstretched muscles

(even if the muscle is a strong one), which in turn keeps injury at bay.

FLEXIBILITY ENHANCERS

#1 Standing Calf Stretch
Position: Face a wall at arm's length, with your hands placed on the wall about twelve inches apart, palms flat at about head level. Place your right foot directly behind the left and at least one foot length apart.

Movement: Lean forward and bend your elbows into the wall until you feel a stretch in the calf of the back leg. Hold for thirty seconds, then repeat with the left leg behind the right.

#2 Full Body Stretch
Position: Lie flat on the floor with your legs together. Relax your arms at your sides.

Movement: Simultaneously stretch your right arm overhead on the floor as you flex your right foot. Hold for

groin. Hold the stretch for thirty seconds.

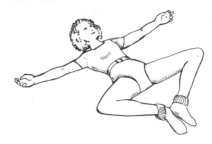

#4 Hamstring Stretch

Position: Sit on the floor with your legs straight and apart in a comfortable V formation.

Movement: Flex your feet so that your toes point up. Place your hands on your right leg as near the ankle as possible. Gently bend over the leg, lowering your head as close to the knee as you can without straining. Hold the stretch for ten seconds, trying to keep the knee as straight as possible. Do not bounce. Return to the starting position and repeat the stretch on the left leg. Repeat three times to each side.

six seconds, then relax the foot as you lower the arm. Repeat on the left side. Repeat four times total.

Note: This elongation movement stretches your arms, shoulders, spine, abdominals, intercostal muscles of the rib cage, feet, and ankles. In fact, it's a great stretch to do in bed in the morning before you plant your feet on the floor.

#3 Groin Stretch

Position: Lie flat with your knees bent and your feet together. Relax your arms at shoulder level or rest your hands on your chest.

Movement: Let your knees fall apart until you feel a mild stretch in the

#5 Upper Body Stretch

Position: Lie on your back, knees bent, feet parallel and hip-width apart. Hold a one- to five-pound weight in both hands (with end facing forward) in front of your body, arms straight. (If you do not have a weight, you can do this same stretch with your hands clasped together.)

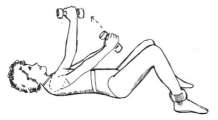

Note: If you're unable to maintain a flat back, take the weight back only as far as you can without lifting your back off the floor.

Movement: Take four slow counts to release the weight back until the tip touches the floor overhead. Then take four counts to bring the weight forward to the starting position. Keep your abdominals pulled in so that your back remains flat on the floor. Exhale back, inhale forward.

▼

"Only years of practice will teach you the mysteries and bold certainty of a real gardener, who treads at random, yet tramples on nothing."

KAREL ČAPEK

TWO

Cultivate the Right Moves

I'm sure you would agree there's no point in having gorgeous garden beds if you have to crawl into yours at the end of the day. Knowing how to make the right moves while you work in the garden pertains not only to strenuous, sweaty chores such as double-digging or hauling a balled scrub across the yard, but also to jobs such as holding a trowel correctly so you don't strain your hand when digging or securing a vine to a trellis top without causing a "pain in the neck."

There is a right and wrong way to move when you garden, and making the right moves makes good garden sense. It's as simple as that. If at day's end, you have trouble straightening up and straightening out (you look and feel like the Hunchback of Notre Dame), it's quite possible you're not aware of the body-racking positions that you assume while you work at your tasks, whether they are strenuous or not.

Unlike other activities or sports in which technique is learned and mastered, most gardeners simply get out there and dig in, so to speak. Although I agree it takes more skill and know-how to sink a hole in one than it does to dig a hole for a delphinium, digging can be hard, particularly when your soil is.

When you learn to ski, for instance, you're shown how to properly plant your poles, but no one tells you how to properly plant your feet when you double-dig or hammer stakes into hard, dry soil. Though sports are taught in a very disciplined way, gardeners are typically on their own in terms of execution, and therein lies the problem.

There's another important reason for cultivating the right moves: when you move correctly, with proper body mechanics, not only do you lessen the stress that would otherwise be placed on muscles and joints, but your movements also become more economical. In other words, you don't have to exert unnecessary energy or effort to accomplish a chore. The sport of gardening is rigorous and sweaty enough; why make it any tougher?

As you read through the following pages that offer guidance and tips, stop and try some of the recommended positions and movement techniques. Once they become second nature, it's easier to put them into play in the garden.

Bending and Lifting

If you're bent out of shape at the end of the day, there's a good chance you're bending incorrectly, particularly when you pick up something bulky or heavy or both. Knowing how to bend over and how to lift an object (or yourself) the correct way is crucial to gardening without taxing your joints and muscles, particularly your back muscles.

Let's say you're picking up a large rock, which you want to move from one spot in your rock garden to another. (Why are we constantly rearranging?) The chance of straining your back is far greater if you neglect to bend your knees. If you keep your knees locked and bend at the hip joint (a common movement mistake), your entire body, particularly your lower back, is placed under stress. The reason for this is that the top of your body is no longer above its support (your feet).

When you bend over with your knees locked, you're actually picking up half your body weight in addition to the weight of the object. When your knees are rigid, your lower-back muscles are put under a damaging load. This sort of misuse, if done regularly, will nearly always lead to back pain or, in extreme cases, to a more severe back condition such as a herniated disk.

On the other hand, studies have shown that lifting heavy objects with the knees bent puts far less pressure on the disks in the vertebral column. (If you observe professional weightlifters, you will notice that they always squat when bending, using mainly their very powerful thigh and buttock muscles and not their back muscles.)

The safe and correct way to bend over when picking up a bulky or heavy object, such as a bag of fertilizer or a filled watering can, is to keep your knees flexed and place

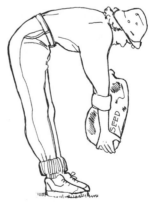

Wrong way to bend and lift

one foot slightly in front of the other, almost as if you're taking a step. Your back should be in an eased and ever so slightly protective curve, not overly rounded, rigid, or stick-straight.

Right way to bend and lift

To avoid straining your back when lifting, bring the object up close to your center. This allows your arms to remain comfortably bent. Lifting anything heavy with your arms fully extended and your

elbows locked stresses the lower back and upper back as well.

When lifting whatever, say a bag of peat moss or lime, your thighs and your abdominal muscles, not your back, should do the heavy work. If you want to garden for years to come without compromising your back, you should do everything possible to develop abdominal and thigh (particularly quadricep) strength.

In fact, all bending movements you make while you carry out your chores should originate with your abdominal muscles pulled in. And I don't mean when you bend over to pick up something heavy. You should try to keep your abdominals contracted whenever you bend over, even if it's just to pick up a pebble or a hand tool. By so doing, your back is guaranteed better protection.

Another way to protect your back when bending over is to make certain that your feet are placed comfortably apart in a stride that's appropriate for you. If you bend over with your feet together and your knees locked, pulling out an unyielding weed for instance, you could strain your back.

In fact, keeping your feet close together when you rake or hoe, for example, not only taxes your back but also limits your range of motion. On the other hand, with your feet comfortably spaced, your balance improves, due to enhanced weight

▼

"Ape" position

distribution, and thus your range of motion is not compromised.

So let's go through the motion of picking up something heavy, a ten-pound bag of manure: First, center yourself in front of the bag. If you're too far away from it, you're going to overstretch your back muscles. You also want to be sure one foot is placed just slightly in front of the other.

Lower your body by bending your knees as you simultaneously pull in your abdomen. You will, in this position, naturally press down on the ball of the forward foot, which will give you additional support and balance. Because you're bending both knees, your (hopefully) strong thigh muscles will pitch in and help out. As you reach for the bag, your arms and shoulders should remain relaxed, never rigid.

Okay, so now you're down with the bag in your hands and it's time to lift it (and yourself) up. When lifting anything heavy, because of the tension created from the weight, the natural tendency is to hold your breath—which is exactly what you do not want. By holding your breath when you exert effort, you create

▼

additional tension in the muscles or, still worse, blood pressure elevation.

Instead, you want to exhale your breath (through your mouth) to reduce the intensity of the lifting process. With the exhalation, you press again on the ball of the forward foot as you stretch your trunk and knees up, returning to an erect posture. Once you're lifted, since you're already in the forward step position, you can then naturally and easily carry the bag of manure (or whatever) forward, keeping it close to your body as you walk. (It might be helpful to try the entire sequence before reading on.)

When chores involve bending over, try working, as I often do, in the "ape" position. To do this, imagine your hip joint as your body's chief spring. You stand with your feet apart and your knees bent slightly. Lean forward, not with your back rounded, but instead with it relatively straight, using your thigh and buttock muscles to lift yourself and the object up. Because your back is not rounded in this particular position, far less stress is placed on it. However, it's still important to keep your abdominal muscles pulled in.

I've noted below a few other lifting tips; please do not take them lightly!

► Do not lift anything heavy if your footing is insecure.

► Do not lift heavy objects over your head.

► Do not lift unbalanced loads, namely, a light load in one arm and a heavy one in the other. Divide appropriately and you will conquer.

► Do not attempt to lift an object (a filled watering can) with one arm while holding on to something else (a bag of potting soil) with the other. Put one down or lift both objects up at the same time to keep your weight evenly distributed and your balance stabilized.

ᴠ ᴠ ᴠ ᴠ ᴠ **TIP** ᴠ ᴠ ᴠ ᴠ ᴠ

To give your legs a workout and aerate your lawn, allowing water, nutrients, and air to reach the roots, take a daily stroll across your lawn in a pair of aerated sandals, available through the A. M. Leonard catalog, which boasts "Sensible Tools for the Serious Gardener." Golf shoes work, too!

Carrying and Holding

So now that you've bent over (properly) and picked the object up, let's carry (no pun intended) this demonstration just a bit further. Correct carrying and holding techniques are also important. They prevent you from overworking your body or, worse, throwing it out of line.

Wrong way to carry objects

Right way to carry objects

When carrying a bag of fertilizer or potting soil, for instance, you should use the strongest and largest joints and muscles (those in your arms) for the job to avoid direct pressure on your smallest joints and weakest muscles (those in your hands and fingers).

This is an important principle to remember if you suffer from arthritic fingers. To lessen the load and avoid taxing your fingers unnecessarily, let your arms assume as much of the burden as possible. Resting the bag on your forearm reduces some of the pressure that would otherwise be placed on your hands and fingers.

Obviously, the large muscles and joints of your arms are better equipped to manage a heavy load than your hand and finger muscles and joints are. In fact, in general, when working in the garden, try to

distribute the weight of any heavy load over as many muscles and joints (knees, hips, back) as possible.

Unlike the deer that roam my property, at times I bite off far more than I can chew. Example: I foolishly attempted to remove a fifty-pound bag of Milorgonite from the back of Old Blue, my Chevy pickup truck. But that wasn't the extent of my stupidity; I then tried to carry the fertilizer to a nearby bed. That was really foolish since my body weight, on a good day, is barely double that of the Milorgonite.

I did have the good sense to drop the load promptly when I realized it was far too heavy for me to carry. When in doubt, let your load out of your grip. That's always a wise move, unless of course you're carrying a delicate piece of garden sculpture, in which case you might have to think twice.

Remember as well that when carrying objects, it's always a better idea to make several trips carrying light loads rather than one back-breaking effort. Better yet, don't carry the load at all, push it in a cart or wheelbarrow.

It's also a good idea to test the waters first: get an idea just how heavy the load is before you attempt to pick it up and carry it anywhere, even to the wheelbarrow or cart. In fact, you should never attempt to carry anything that's heavy until you have tested its weight first and tested to see how it's going to sag or shift as you carry it.

By all means, avoid carrying anything heavy if you have a serious back problem or have sustained a back injury. Instead of getting immediate gratification, get assistance! Granted, it might mean waiting patiently and not getting the task done on the spot, but it might also save you a trip to the chiropractor. It's far easier to prevent injuries in the garden than to recover from them.

Patience is a virtue that pays off in the garden too, so don't even try to haul or carry anything heavy if you're rushed; you're more apt to injure yourself. In gardening, slower and gentler become desired traits; gardening should be an ongoing pleasure not an on the spot emergency! Besides, there's *always* more to do; that's the nature of the sport.

There's another aspect to carrying objects correctly. Let's say you have to carry a watering can across the lawn, which is something I end up doing quite frequently. That's because I wind in the hose at the end of the day, then decide I absolutely must transplant something else. Naturally, that something else needs to be watered. So I fill the watering can to capacity and haul it across the lawn and up the hill to (naturally) one of the most remote spots in the garden.

Carrying a heavy watering can, or anything heavy for that matter, in one hand not only taxes the arm and shoulder but also causes a balance problem since one side of the body has weight pulling down on it while the other does not. What tends to happen is your body gives in to the downward pull by sagging or by displacing one hip out to the side. This is stressful not only to the hip but to the back as well. In addition, when one side of the body is pulled down and out of line, your balance is compromised, which means you could trip or fall.

One way to get around this problem, somewhat, is to switch hands from time to time. If you're carrying a heavy pail full of water in your right hand, stop as soon as you begin to experience fatigue in the arm. Rest the pail on the ground, take a deep breath, then lift the pail up with your left hand. This way

▽ ▽ ▽ ▽ ▽ ▽ ▽ ▽ ▽ ▽ ▽ ▽ ▽ **TIP** ▽ ▽ ▽ ▽ ▽ ▽ ▽ ▽ ▽ ▽ ▽ ▽ ▽ ▽

Getting sliced by a lawn mower blade and being hit by rocks, pebbles, or other propelled objects are two of the most common lawn mower-related injuries. (Mower blades, rotating at nearly 200 miles per hour, can turn seemingly harmless sticks and stones into dangerous missiles when they are picked up and hurled at that speed.)

Here are a few tips for mowing safely.

► Before you start to mow, clear the lawn of sticks, stones, toys, garden hoses, and so forth.

► Wear sturdy shoes with sure-grip soles, slacks rather than shorts, and no voluminous sleeves or dangling jewelry.

► Wear safety goggles to protect your eyes and ear protectors to protect your hearing and ward off headaches. Both items are available through garden supply catalogs.

► When operating a walk-behind mower, cut across slopes, not up and down, to minimize the risk of the mower rolling back. For a riding mower, do the opposite to reduce the risk of tipping sideways.

► Clear the yard of rocks, sticks, and other objects that can be turned into missiles by mower blades. A walk-behind mower should always be equipped with a rear skirt to protect your legs from flying objects.

► Look several feet ahead when mowing.

► Refuel only when the engine is cool—never while a mower is running since gas is highly flammable.

► Keep children and pets out of the yard when mowing.

your right side has a chance to recover before it takes on the load again.

And that's precisely why you should try to develop some amount (even if it's minimal) of ambidexterity. If you can occasionally use your less favored hand, the more favored one has a chance to rest and recover.

There's more to carrying objects safely and correctly: don't trip yourself up by blocking your view. This can easily happen when you're carrying something that's too tall, like a lilac bush. (There I was hauling "Miss Kim" across my lawn, that was until I tripped over the ceramic toad that was hidden between the hostas.) When carrying anything in the garden, maintain an unobstructed view.

On the subject of obstructions, the garden is filled with them, some of which God put there, like brooks and boulders for instance, and others that you put there, like benches, birdbaths, bridges, and other garden decorations. They all have the potential to get in your way, particularly if you have a habit of moving into reverse before looking behind you.

Every gardener has a story about backing into something or other, but when that something is a rosebush, or that other is stinging nettle, it can be a painful experience. Remember, look over your shoulder before you go into reverse.

Reaching

Another motion with the potential for stress and fatigue, not only on the back but on your shoulders and arms as well, occurs when you strain to reach too far, be it overhead, to the side, or simply in front of you. Naturally, if your range of motion is good, meaning if you're agile and flexible, it's easier to reach in any direction without overly taxing your muscles.

But if you have to prune the upper branches of an overgrown shrub and you're unable to reach it comfortably, straining to do so can be stressful to your arms and neck. So what should you do aside from having someone taller do the job for you?

Instead of straining your neck by cocking your head back or overworking your arms to reach a spot that's really not within comfortable range, take the time to take out the ladder. Remember to carry it with care, meaning in both hands. And don't even consider climbing it unless your hands are free. In fact, it's always a good idea to have someone assist you. This way, the "grounded" person can hand you what you need and keep an eye on your movements and balance (or lack of it). Make sure also that your ladder is stable and safely positioned. Do not use a ladder to reach anything if the ladder's placement is at all questionable; a wobbly ladder can cause the downfall of even the most well-balanced, graceful gardener.

As for correct reaching technique, there is a right and wrong way to reach, too. If you have to raise your arms overhead, to pull down an invasive vine for instance, you want to involve your shoulders as well as your arms. It makes good movement sense not to overuse one area (your arms) if another area (your shoulders) can pitch in to help.

I'll give you another example: Instead of using only your hand to weed, which places stress on the muscles and joints, try instead to incorporate your entire arm in the weeding motion to make it a fuller,

▼

▽ ▽ ▽ ▽ ▽ **TIP** ▽ ▽ ▽ ▽ ▽

Take care: Leaves allowed to accumulate on sloping driveways and walkways get dangerously slippery when wet.

more fluid movement. Don't just grab the weed with your clenched hand; let your arm give your hand a hand.

When reaching to work overhead—let's say you're securing a flowering vine to a trellis top or a bird feeder to a high branch—don't keep your arms raised for too long; lower them as soon as you feel any strain or fatigue coming on. Or better yet, don't wait for the fatigue to set in, relax your arms by lowering them for a minute and shaking them out.

Pushing

When pushing heavy loads in a wheelbarrow or cart, use more than just your arms and hands for muscle power; your legs (that's exactly why it's important to strengthen your quadriceps) should also assume some of the load. By keeping your knees flexed as you push, your strong thigh muscles can pitch in and help out. You also want to keep your abdominal muscles pulled in (I know I sound like a broken record) for added back protection.

Whenever pushing or pulling a heavy load, whether across the yard or up a hill, keep your breathing smooth and fluid. As I mentioned earlier, we tend to hold our breath when we exert effort, which only makes a task more difficult. Since pushing anything uphill is more strenuous than pushing on level ground, you don't want to rob yourself of energy by not breathing correctly.

If you feel like you're straining when, for instance, you're pushing a cart filled with plant matter across the yard, don't push yourself. Taking on more than you can manage is not smart gardening. And when it comes to pushing a heavy load, you certainly don't want to risk injuring your back. If you find the load is too heavy to handle, let someone else take the handles, someone who can manage the push with less difficulty. There's nothing wrong with asking for help when you need it; what is wrong is *not* asking.

As far as what to push, if it's a choice between a wheelbarrow or a cart with two large rubber wheels, my preference is a cart. The initial expense might be greater, but so will your control and mobility. Carts tend to carry far more than the traditional wheelbarrow, with less back-breaking effort. And carts are better balanced. As you might know from experience, there's nothing more frustrating than filling a wheelbarrow with leaves, soil, pebbles, or whatever, only to have it topple over

When I made my switch years ago from a small, red wheelbarrow to a big black cart, gardening reached yet another level of portability. The cart gives me lots of room to carry my supplies (plant and personal) from spot to spot without having to constantly run back into the house or garage. Besides all my gardening gear and equipment, my cart totes my white-and-green L. L. Bean bag that holds my water bottle, sunblock, bug repellent, a wide-brimmed hat or sun visor, a hand towel to blot my brow, sunglasses, and always some fresh fruit to snack on.

While we're on the subject, in the summer, excessive perspiration can result in a loss of potassium, which can easily lead to muscle cramping, so I snack on a banana, apple, grapes, watermelon slices or some dried apricots and raisins, all of which pack a potassium wallop and can easily be enjoyed right in the

> ▽ ▽ ▽ ▽ ▽ **TIP** ▽ ▽ ▽ ▽ ▽
>
> When working near brambles or anything that could injure your eyes, protect them by wearing glasses with wraparound lenses.

garden while I work. Or I might stop for a cool garden "cocktail," which I whip up in the blender and either enjoy in the house or in the garden while I take a refueling break. (Recipes are on pages 84–85.)

As to what else goes into the cart, I can tell you what does not—a phone. For me, phone calls are like invasive weeds. Intruders! When I'm in my garden, I want my ears to relax along with the rest of me.

Dragging and Pulling

I first became acquainted with the drag-the-blanket approach to raking leaves many years ago when I picked up Ruth Stout's excellent book on mulch gardening, *How to Have a Green Thumb without an Aching Back* (Galahad Books). This back-saving method for debris removal involves raking leaves onto a big blanket, sheet, or tarp. Once it's full, all you have to do is take the four corners and hold them together to form a big pouch. Now, with the blanket in front of you, move backwards, dragging it to a spot in the garden where you want to deposit the leaves.

This back-saving strategy works not only for leaves but for any raked-up matter (such as pine needles) that you want to drag to a disposal site. Since you're moving backwards, take care not to crash into anything behind you—like a tree.

Also, when moving backwards and dragging anything in front of you, avoid rounding your back too much, which stresses the lumbar (lower) spine. Remember as well that your back will be better protected when dragging whatever if you keep your knees flexed and your abdominal muscles pulled in (here I go again).

Another way to drag the leaves after you've raked them onto the blanket is to take hold of two corners in each hand and drag the blanket *behind* you to the disposal site. To protect your back when pulling anything behind you (the hose, cart, wheelbarrow), keep your shoulders squared off (don't twist from the waist) for proper weight distribu-

tion. That means face directly forward as you move, whether you're pulling the load with one hand or both hands.

Remember as well that dragging heavy or bulky objects has the potential for causing not only arm strain but shoulder and neck tension, too. This occurs when you pull something that's really too heavy for you to comfortably manage or simply when you use more effort than necessary. So try to avoid tightening and tensing your shoulders when pulling or dragging any-

▼

thing heavy. If you find your shoulders are hiked up toward your ears, that's a sure indication that you're overworking them and should lower them to a more comfortable, neutral position.

Another mistake made when dragging anything heavy is locking the elbow of the arm(s) that's pulling. This can be potentially injurious if you do it too often because locking the elbows (like locking the knees) places excessive stress on the elbow joint and could eventually result in tendinitis.

When pushing, pulling, or dragging something, use your entire body, especially the weight and strength of your trunk and legs, as the energy source. This applies not only to pulling a heavy load but to pulling out resistant weeds as well. To manage the tough weeding with a minimum of effort, stand with your feet around the roots, then bend your knees, keeping your back as straight as possible. Let your legs assist your arms in the pulling

process. With each tug, blow out your breath; it makes it easier. Remember, it's better to attack stubborn weeds when the ground is moist, so give the area a light hosing before you even attempt to yank weeds out.

▼

"Gardens are not made . . . by singing . . . "Oh, how beautiful!" and sitting in the shade."

RUDYARD KIPLING

▲

Ground Work

SQUATTING, SITTING, KNEELING

Positioning your body properly when you do work close to or on the ground is important, particularly for the sake of your back. Squatting, sitting, or working on your hands and knees to weed, for instance, is far less taxing on the back than standing up and bending over from your waist.

Working in a squat position can actually be very lengthening for your back, provided you squat the right way. Always avoid remaining in a squat for too long, though. Also, do not squat at all if you have knee problems; squatting can further stress your knees by overstretching the ligaments.

If you do squat for ground work, weeding or sowing seeds for instance, you want to keep your back relatively straight, both knees bent, and your buttocks lowered close to the ground. To reduce stress on your knees, your heels should remain *flat* not lifted.

If a full-squat is not comfortable, you can do a semicrouch by placing one knee on the ground. Other options to squatting are working on your hands and knees (knee pads come in handy for this), or sitting at ground level, providing you face the direction of your work. If you twist and turn, you stress the lower back, particularly if you twist abruptly.

Learning to squat comfortably may take a bit of practice indoors before you can manage it with ease in the garden. There are various

ways to practice. One way to develop "squat skill" is to do the following: Squat with your feet flat and your toes pointed out at approximately fifteen-degree angles; your heels should be about a foot apart. This squat position stretches the front part of the lower legs, the knees, back, ankles, Achilles tendons, and the groin muscles.

Begin by holding this position for as little as eight or ten seconds. Make certain that you keep your knees to the outside of your shoulders and directly above the big toes. As you gain flexibility and control, you will be able to comfortably hold the position longer and to lower yourself into a deeper squat as well.

When you first practice the squat, there may be a problem with balance, usually falling backwards because of tight ankles and tight Achilles tendons. If you're unable to squat without support, there are two other ways of practicing it. One way is by leaning your back against a wall.

To do this, stand with your feet about five inches from the wall, arms relaxed at your sides or resting on your thighs. Then lower your body to a half squat as you press

▼

your back against the wall. Work up to maintaining the position for thirty seconds.

Another way of practicing the squat is by holding on to something approximately waist high, like a heavy piece of furniture or a railing. (Whatever you use, make sure it's anchored in place or so heavy that it could not possibly move.) For this exercise, stand tall, feet comfortably apart, while holding on to your support. Then lower your body by bending your knees, going only halfway down. Do not even attempt to do a complete knee bend. After you lower yourself, come back up slowly. (You might want to try out the various squat positions before reading on.)

As you practice this half-squat, remember to keep your back straight and your chin level. You can gradually increase the number of repetitions until you've worked up to a comfortable dozen.

The best way to get up from a squat (whether you practice it in the house or actually do it in the garden) is to pull in your abdominals, keeping your back as straight as possible, and lift from your legs, not from your back.

In the garden, when I squat to plant or to weed, I generally line my feet up, one with the other, about twelve inches apart. Or I might squat with one foot just slightly in front of the other (with the heel of the back foot slightly lifted), which also feels comfortable. Both positions allow freedom and ease of motion in my upper body. I can quite easily swivel from my hips, reaching to either side, or I can stretch my entire body forward without straining my back. But I make it a point not to remain in a squat for too long. When my knees begin to feel at all fatigued, I immediately stand up to shake out my legs.

Another option for doing ground work is to sit on a cushion or on a wooden stool. Make certain, however, that your cushion or stool is as close to your work as possible so that you don't have to lean too far forward; the straighter you hold your spine, the less strain you place on it.

According to my dad, who still works in his garden at the age of eighty-four, the Grass Hopper, a multipurposed, lightweight work clothesline rope attached to this stool allows me to carry it around the garden, even when my hands are full. I just sling it over my shoulder (or I put it in the cart), and it goes wherever I go.

A kneeling stool, available at most garden supply stores or through catalogs, is yet another option for ground work. Many of my more "mature" friends swear by them, particularly those who are unable to get up and down from the ground easily due to arthritic knees. These convenient stools are usually made with raised, curved end bars, and come in handy when you're lowering or lifting yourself. If you suffer from arthritic knees, this convenient piece of garden "furniture" makes kneeling far less troublesome. And there's yet a bonus: Inverted, the kneeler becomes a handy seat.

If you suffer from arthritic fingers, when you get up from the ground, do not place unnecessary weight on your finger joints, particularly the thumb, which is very vulnerable. Instead, push yourself away from the ground, not by leaning on your fingers, but by leaning on the heel of your hands.

seat on wheels (manufactured by Step 2), has been a back-saver for him. This handy item, ideal for the more seasoned gardener, is sold at garden centers as well as at large hardware stores that feature gardening equipment.

My own gardening cushion is an old black meditation pillow (from my flower child days), which happens to be just the right size and shape for my less than ample derriere. When the ground is wet, I sit on a low, sturdy, little wooden stool that I found at a tag sale in Copake, New York. A loop of

Turning Compost

Years ago, my friend Reggie built me a three-compartment compost bin, adapted from one illustrated in *Crockett's Flower Garden* (Little

Brown) on page 297. Although hardly fancy, this no-frills setup works just fine and has held up beautifully. I like it because it's unobtrusive, not some huge, black-plastic eyesore that wrecks the view. Mine sits in a sunny spot just beyond my woodland garden. And it's easy to get to. (There's just no way I would compost if I had to lug my kitchen remains halfway across the yard.)

Turning the compost can be stressful on the back, so I never make a project of it. Instead, I devote several minutes to it over the course of each weekend, which is not very time-consuming and doesn't tire me out. By breaking up the task, it gets done without my back getting done in.

As for the most back-saving way to manage the chore (short of having someone else do it) when using a pitchfork, you have to bend your knees when you plunge the tool into the compost and bend them again when lifting the loaded pitchfork. If your legs really "pitch" in, and your abdominal muscles are held in, your back will not be unnecessarily taxed.

You also want to distribute the weight of the pitchfork (or whatever tool you use) as evenly as possible in both hands. Like other movements, this one benefits from being done smoothly and slowly.

If you're moving the compost from one spot to another (and this holds true when you're moving soil

or sod), the turning motion should be made with your entire body. Swivel on your feet, and face in the direction the compost is going. Avoid twisting from the waist only, which can potentially injure the back, particularly if you twist abruptly.

▼

"I am a lazy gardener, subscribing to the view that no man should have a garden larger than his wife can take care of."

FREDERICK McGOURTY

Digging

When using a spade or pitchfork for digging, you want to work with the tool as close to your body as possible so that you don't overuse your back by bending too far forward. In fact, you should plant your feet not only comfortably apart but also close to the hole you're digging. You should also keep your knees relaxed (never locked) so that your range of motion is not compromised when you lift the sod or soil.

When you dig with a shovel or spade, or even a light hand-held tool, such as a trowel, try not to grip the handle of the tool with too much intensity. Tightening excessively, and thus tensing the hand muscles unnecessarily, not only stresses them but fatigues the entire arm as well.

▼

"You're supposed to get tired planting bulbs. But it's an agreeable tiredness."
GAIL GODWIN

▲

Raking

One way to make raking less taxing and tiring (aside from using a leaf blower) is to switch your hand positions on the rake handle (right lower than left or vice versa) and to switch the rake from one side of your body to the other. In other words, if you begin with the rake on the right side of your body, and the left hand below the right on the rake handle, after several minutes, to reduce the workload on the right side, switch the rake to the left side and place your right hand below the left on the handle. Use this side switching and hand switching when you work with a hoe or a long-handled weeder as well. Try to use the tool on both sides of your body instead of favoring one side only.

"In the spring, at the end of the day, you should smell like dirt."

MARGARET ATWOOD

Energy Preservation

THE RHYTHM METHOD

A good tennis serve or golf swing requires a rhythm, as do gardening chores. Edging beds, raking, hoeing, and so forth should be done, if possible, with flow and rhythm. Gardening by the "rhythm method" is all about moving smoothly—with care, control, and a sense of pace and timing. By moving this way, you will not only preserve your energy, but you will also protect your muscles and joints from overexertion and undue stress.

Let's take edging a bed for instance. When you press your foot against the edger, try not to push your foot down too forcefully, abruptly, or rapidly. Keep the motion as smooth and fluid as possible. By moving your leg with care, in a rhythm that's comfortable for you, far less strain is placed on the leg muscles, particularly the calves, which really get a workout when you use an edger.

Or take another example. It's easier to prune or clip away at a hedge when you establish a smooth, comfortable pace. Instead of rapidly and forcefully working the shears or pruners nonstop until you have to stop because your arms ache, a better method would be to clip eight times, lower your arms to rest them, then repeat the same sequence until the job is completed. Working this way (clip/rest) lets you establish a pace and flow. Yes, it slows you down somewhat, but this is beneficial because working too rapidly can deplete your energy.

Gardening is no different from other activities or sports. Your movements can't have a comfortable flow if you hold your breath while you work. Chest breathing, stomach breathing, deep breathing, shallow breathing—it doesn't matter as long as you _are_ breathing. And why would you want to hold your breath in your fragrant garden anyway?

Muscles feel less fatigued if you maintain a steady breathing pattern while you work, turning the

▽ ▽ ▽ ▽ ▽ **TIP** ▽ ▽ ▽ ▽ ▽

Birds, bees, and butterflies all bring rhythm and movement into the garden. Easy maintenance plants for attracting bees and butterflies are bee balm, catnip, valerian, rosemary, and chives. Hummingbirds (talk about rhythm) are attracted to red flowers. Geraniums, hibiscus, trumpet vine, and monarda are just some of their favorites.

compost, digging, or pulling out weeds. Try to accompany the exertion phase of any movement with an exhalation of breath. Let me give you an example: If you're hammering stakes into the ground to support your tomato plants, you should exhale your breath with each downward motion of the hammer, when the intensity of the movement is greatest. By breathing correctly, that is, exhaling during the effort phase of a movement, tension that you might be holding in your body, no matter what the task is, will be reduced—or better yet, eliminated entirely.

ECONOMY OF MOVEMENT

Being economical about your moves also makes sense and saves energy. Economy of movement while gardening means making your chores simpler. If you're working on the ground, make it easy for yourself by keeping your tools close at hand so you don't have to turn or twist for them unnecessarily. Not only will this save energy, but as I previously mentioned, twisting motions, particularly when done quickly, can overload the muscles, which can then result in muscle strain.

Timing your work wisely is another way to preserve energy and make your movements more economical. It's less of a chore to plant anything (stakes included) when the earth is moist and slightly soft rather than hard, dry, and dusty. On the other hand, you don't want to dig immediately after a long and heavy rainfall when the soil forms into mud balls as you squeeze some in your fist.

Here's another means of timing for energy preservation: It takes less effort to work when the sun is less intense. Not only is overexposure to the sun potentially dangerous, but gardening during the heat of the day can also be debilitating. Plan strenuous projects when conditions in the garden are working with, not against, you.

Also, plan ahead. To keep the deer from devouring my garden, my final Sunday afternoon ritual before heading back to Manhattan was to scatter Milorgonite (biosolid waste from Milwaukee) around the beds. Deer are supposed to be put off by this gray, gritty fertilizer that's far from fragrant. The scattering process was somewhat time-consuming and not one of my favorite chores. Now, instead of making a project of it, I keep a pail of Milorgonite in my cart so that during the weekend, I scatter it wherever I happen to be working, thus saving time and unnecessary steps. (Despite my efforts, though, the deer still eat everything!)

Unnecessary effort also occurs when you grip a tool with too much tension and pressure. Again, make your movements economical; using excessive strength is not an energy-saving way to handle a tool. Your grip should be firm but never tense and rigid. Once you're aware that you're exerting too much effort, you're more apt to ease up. But first must come the awareness.

Another way to move economically is to alternate heavy or repeated tasks with easy, less fatiguing chores. This allows your muscles time to recover before they get too weary.

For instance, you might take a break from raking leaves to cut flowers for a fall bouquet. Or, having turned the compost, you might turn your body away from the heap and move toward the house for a healthy snack or well-deserved nap. Now that's what I call an energy-saving move when you're too pooped to plant.

"A garden is like those pernicious machineries which catch a man's coat-skirt or his hand, and draw in his arm, his leg, and his whole body to irresistible destruction."

RALPH WALDO EMERSON

Tools and Attire

It's tough to cultivate the right moves if you're working with the wrong tools. The tool should be appropriate not only for the task, but also for the person using it. In other words, the hoe that's comfortable for your hardy, 200-pound husband is not the right hoe for 100-pound, petite you.

Naturally, the larger the person, the larger and heavier the tool can be. Trowels, rakes, hoes, indeed, any hand tool, should be tested and weighed before buying it. The length, overall size, and balance must be comfortable for you because a tool can either sabotage your work or make it infinitely easier. If you are tall, always purchase long-handled tools; four-foot handles are simply too short for a person taller than six feet. To find a good selection of long-handled tools, you might want to check the A. M. Leonard catalog, one of my favorite tool sources.

Before purchasing, for instance, a spade or shovel, you should first go through the motions of digging with the tool to get an idea whether it's too light or too heavy, or whether the balance feels right for you. Don't be reticent or shy about picking it up and going through the motions at the garden center or wherever you do your purchasing. You wouldn't think twice about swinging a tennis racket and testing it for comfort and weight in the store; the same holds true for a tool before you purchase it. Remember, try it before you buy it!

Once you practice using a tool long enough, it will become

automatic, a habit. And it will become a good or bad habit depending on how you learn to use and handle it from the start. You know the old expression, "Habits are easy to make but hard to break." That certainly holds true for how you hold and handle your garden tools.

Even if you do have the right tools, if they are not maintained in good working condition, you can't expect to make the right moves. Digging and cutting tools will not perform effectively if the working edges are blunted with caked soil or rust. Sharp tools mean less sweat in the garden—it's as simple as that. To keep tools in good working order, you can hone the edges with a standard metal file, whetstone, or grinding wheel. To ward off rust, clean and dry all your tools after use and wipe them with an oily rag.

It's trite but true: You get what you pay for. A traditional wood and forged-steel hand tool is well worth its price and will last for many years with proper care. The quality of the tool determines not only the quality of the work but also the quality of the experience. Really fine tools do cost more, but they are better balanced and easier to wield and, therefore, less tiring and thus more economical to use.

In addition, when a tool is well-made, the handles fit your hands better, which not only keeps your hands from overworking but protects them from painful blisters. What's more, good tools are made from superior steel, so a premium tool's cutting edges are easier to sharpen and stay sharp longer.

Remember, dampness is a hand tool's worst enemy. To keep them in top shape, don't put them away caked with dirt. Knock off loose dirt, then plunge the tool up and down in a bucket filled with builder's sand moistened with motor oil. Wipe off the oil with a cloth and store the tool in a dry place.

When purchasing tools, look for unpainted, oiled, or varnished handles of white ash or birch, wood with a straight, tight grain. These will stay smoothest with wear. To keep the handles from drying out during the garden season, apply natural oils to them (olive oil works well). When you put them away for the winter, apply a coat of linseed oil to the wood, or you can lightly sand and revarnish the handles. Come spring, your hands will thank you for the care your tools received before their hibernation.

It's also tough to cultivate the right moves if you wear the wrong attire. Now, I'm not talking about sprucing up in fancy garden clothes. Personally, I'm happy as a clematis when I garden in my denim overalls (they have lots of big pockets), which I bought years ago in the kids' department at the Gap.

What I mean by wrong attire is

clothing that limits your range of motion. Skin-tight jeans with no breathing space, for instance, will not allow you to move with ease and comfort, not to mention breathe with ease—and we know how essential that is. Speaking of jeans or trousers, cuffless ones are best since cuffs catch soil and sneak it into the house where you do not want it.

There's something else to be said about the clothing you wear, again not in terms of what's chic and current but what's safe and smart. Cuffs and sleeves on loose, baggy garments could become entangled in moving parts of machines, so be smart about what you wear when operating machinery of any kind.

Also, for the sake of safety and health, keep your skin under wraps, not only to avoid excessive sun exposure (particularly if you're not prudent about applying sunscreen), but also to keep the ticks from attacking. The more you cover, the less territory they can claim. As for fabrics, in warm weather, there's nothing quite like good old fashioned cotton for perspiration absorption. It also launders well, certainly a factor to consider.

Shoes will also smuggle soil into the house, so take them off at the door. Here's a helpful note: What you put on your feet counts every bit as much as how you plant them when you dig, hoe, rake, and so forth. I'm exceedingly attached to

my yellow, rubber garden shoes, particularly in the summer when my feet call out for an on-the-spot spritzing. They're perfectly adequate for light garden work, but not for chores that require heavy-duty leg and foot work. When I really need foot (and back) protection, I wear my canvas and leather Timberland boots.

Thin rubber shoes, tired and torn sneakers, sandals, and other lightweight footwear simply cannot stand (no pun intended) much digging or strenuous leg work. For the sake of your feet, wear footwear with thick rubber soles. Proper cushioning not only protects your feet but, equally important, lessens the stress and impact on your back as well. And when I say "thick," I mean thick enough to absorb the repeated shocks of a spade or shovel. (And thick enough to stop a shovel or hoe that wants to dig your toes instead of the soil.) If you properly care for your feet (with support and cushioning), they will be willing and able to stand up to long hours in the garden, so choose your footwear wisely.

▽ ▽ ▽ ▽ ▽ **TIP** ▽ ▽ ▽ ▽ ▽

To spot the worn trowel dropped in the perennial border or the rake left on the lawn, paint bright-orange stripes on the wooden handles of your tools so that they will pop right out of the grass or wherever you left them when you went into the house for a pit stop. Bright adhesive tape does the same trick if paint is not feasible.

Going without socks invites corns and blisters, so I generally wear a thin pair of cotton socks (even when I wear my rubber shoes) not only for foot protection but also for perspiration absorption. In addition, for the sake of tick control, socks make sense since ankles are one spot they really like.

There's something else that I wear (use is more like it) to assure that I make the right moves, particularly on days when my back feels somewhat iffy. Years ago, I had the misfortune to be in the way of a New York cab driver who ran a red light and ran me down in the process. So when my back feels vulnerable, out comes "Old Reliable," my lumbar corset. Not only does it hold my back in line, but it also holds me back from attempting the more brutish feats of gardening when I really should behave myself.

You can purchase a corset, such as the model (1079) I wear manufactured by Bell-Horn, at most surgical or medical supply stores. They're sized (small, medium, and large) and have velcro straps that allow for ease of entry and exit. (This feature is particularly meaningful if you drink lots of fluids while you garden.) If you decide to purchase a corset and wear it occasionally because your back is your Achilles heel, purchase one that is constructed with metal, not plastic, stays for maximum support.

Wearing the appropriate gloves for a particular task can also make your moves more comfortable and correct. For instance, certain gloves can actually assist your movements by providing traction on a tool handle. I'm referring to the type of glove readily available in hardware stores and garden supply centers. These gloves are constructed of heavy, unbleached cotton, with rubber or vinyl dots spaced evenly over the gripping surface. The dots greatly improve traction when using tools, even when they're wet.

THREE
▽▽▽▽▽▽

Stop ... Stretch ... and Smell the Roses

Pacing yourself, and knowing when to take a break for a stretch or breather, is far more important than knowing the Latin name for lamb's ear or the difference between hot and cold compost. So here's a horticultural mantra to chant while you plant: "Don't kvetch. Stop and stretch!"

While you work at your chores, your body (not unlike your plants) sends out signals—these signals should be heeded. Instead of holding out until you can't straighten out (or up) because you've been locked in a position for too long, garden sense says stop for a stretch from time to time.

Gardening without occasional time-outs can potentially tax your muscles and joints; this is true even if you're agile and limber. Just think about it: some of the twisted and distorted positions you end up in (often with your end up) are nothing less than acrobatic feats. But these posi-

tions can stress and strain your body.

That's only part of the problem. Muscular fatigue and soreness also result from remaining in one position for too long or from repeating the same movement over and over, such as clenching your hand when you weed. And that's exactly why my rule of thumb (green or otherwise) is this: from time to time stop gardening and start stretching.

During peak season when there's so much to do, the tendency is to overdo (translation: wreck and ravage your body). This is common practice, in particular, when one owns a weekend property. (Weekend gardeners can, indeed, be maniacal.) Believe me, I know it's difficult to manage everything in a mere two days. The pileup of chores can be awesome—weeds to be pulled, edges to be defined, slugs to be evicted, and on and on. One could garden from dawn to dusk and still never get it all done.

But getting it done should not be the objective. This is what I constantly remind myself. According to my wise friend Ciba, who attempts (with only moderate success) to keep my compulsive nature in check, "Gardening is a work in progress." If you can manage to keep this in mind ("Needlepoint it on a pillow," says she), your garden can be that special, wonderful place for recovering your bearings not losing them.

So here are two questions: Do you periodically take time out from your chores just to sit back and admire your work? Do you occasionally stop for a replenishing breath or a de-kinking stretch? If you don't allow for these important time-outs, you really should; gardening should nourish not drain you. Not only will a brief break give you time to recharge your batteries for still more tasks, but a short time out allows you the well-deserved opportunity to rest, reflect, and enjoy the fruits (and flowers) of your labor.

Let me give you a personal example: It's a glorious July morning and I'm working in my little herb garden attired in my appropriately dirty overalls. The birds are singing, there's a pungent scent of basil in the air, and life in the Berkshires is just about as good as it gets. But instead of being "in the moment" (praising myself for the parsley that has escaped the ravages of the Hillsdale rabbit population), I'm thinking about all the "elsewheres" that need my attention—the wilting snapdragons, the morning glories under beetle siege, the loosestrife robbing the phlox of their rightful territory. Sound familiar?

This is no way to garden sanely. To quote Ciba, "You can't let the pileup of projects put you over the lunatic fringe." She is right. Gardening should relax, renew, and revive you, not exhaust, drain, or overwhelm you.

If you feel rushed and anxious to get it all done, and you assume more than you can comfortably manage, not only do you miss out on the pleasures of the moment, but equally important, you might miss out on the signals your body is sending you: an ache in the elbow or strain in the neck, for instance. We take signals from our flowers when they speak to us (water me, divide me, stake me), and that's a good thing, but we often ignore the signals from our bodies, and that's not a good thing.

Take time out. Stretch, take a revitalizing deep breath, or change tasks to utilize your muscles in a different way and thus not overwork them. Instead of weeding for an entire morning, which involves a tiring and repetitive arm and hand motion, alternate weeding with a beetle attack. By switching activities in such a way, you give your muscles time to rest.

Let me give you a few simple, sample time-outs: In the fall, when I'm busy putting my garden to bed, I also have to contend with the gazillion spring bulbs I ordered in a moment of utter madness. As you know, one does not plant a mere dozen bulbs, hundreds is more like it. Needless to say, planting bushels of bulbs can be taxing, not only on your bulb budget, but on your wrists and hands as well.

So at fifteen-minute intervals, when my hands begin to protest, instead of continuing to work, I give my hands a brief rest. I stop planting, remove my gloves, and vigorously shake out my hands a few times, first in front of my body at chest level, then overhead. This easy shake-out not only relaxes the muscles in the wrists but revs up circulation in the fingers as well.

If my forearm feels tired from the continual motion of plunging the bulb planter into the soil, I might do the following: With my fingers interlaced, I straighten my arms in front at chest level, pressing my palms forward. Not only does the forearm derive a good stretch from this simple motion, but the wrists and fingers relax, too. And I can easily do this stretch while seated on the ground or while standing.

Having worked for perhaps an hour or longer, instead of planting

still more bulbs, I'll take on a chore that's less fatiguing on my hands, or I might just stop for several minutes, stretch out on the grass, and admire my work. Feeling particularly virtuous about all the bulbs that have reached their final resting place, I might pat myself on my back, which literally is a good exercise for the hands and fingers!

Generally, when chores have me grounded (and my back rounded), I make it a point to stand up from time to time just to do something basic like shaking out my arms or my legs. Or I might just jog in place for a minute to rev up the circulation in my legs, particularly if I've been working on the ground with my legs folded underneath me.

Or when I'm on my knees weeding in all sorts of pretzel-like positions, I periodically stand up and do the following: With my feet about shoulder-width apart, I extend my arms toward the sky. Then I slowly stretch, first with one arm, then with the other, reaching higher and higher (as if I'm picking apples off a tree). This easy-to-do movement feels great and stretches me from my fingertips all the way down to my waist. Once I've done my "apple picking" for as little as a minute, I'm ready to resume my weeding with added energy.

there's no tension whatsoever on the back of my neck.

My exuberance for gardening bloomed into pure and utter passion in no time. I confess my possessed behavior has resulted in such questionable acts as whispering sweet nothings to my nasturtium or making midnight inspection (by flashlight) when I arrive late on Friday night. But these actions probably don't surprise you at all.

Gardening can trigger not only weird but relentless and obsessive behavior. We become so involved in what we're doing we often ignore the "help" signals our body sends out, such as knee discomfort from squatting for too long or neck pain from cocking the head back too far and too long. If you really want to garden comfortably, as well as for years to come, these significant signals from your significant body should not be overlooked or ignored.

Another thing I might do after I've been grounded for a while is just stand up and hang loose like a rag doll. With my feet about six to eight inches apart and parallel, I bend my knees, lower my head, and let my upper body (pelvis, rib cage, and head) round forward, with my arms hanging limply. In this position, the front of my torso is close to my thighs, which means my back is fairly rounded. To protect my back while it stretches out, which takes no more than ten seconds, I keep my knees flexed, my abdominal muscles pulled in, and my chin tucked so

The easy take-a-break stretches that I recommend you do while you garden require minimum time and effort. The purpose of these mini-movements is not to tone and tighten your trouble spots, but to relax and soothe the spots that get into trouble while you work at your chores.

You probably know the spots I mean all too well. Because of the strange and wacky positions you endlessly get into, and because of the repetitive movements you make, your back, shoulders, neck, arms, and hands are prime areas for overwork, strain, and fatigue.

"Working in the garden gives me a profound feeling of inner peace. Nothing here is in a hurry. There is no rush toward accomplishment, no blowing of trumpets.... Everything is changing, growing, aiming at something, but silently, unboastfully, taking its time."

RUTH STOUT

What follows are a selection of relaxing, de-kinking movements that I've personally tried and tested in my garden. I'm pleased to report they tested positive, meaning they work on tired muscles and overworked joints. Best of all, you can do them quickly and almost effortlessly and hardly miss a beat.

While you read through this section of the book, it might be helpful to stop occasionally to give these simple stretches a try. By becoming familiar with them, it is hoped you will remember to do them from time to time while you go about your tasks and chores.

Time-Out

FOR YOUR BACK AND SHOULDERS

Let's begin with back fatigue that results, for instance, when you work in a forward bend for an extended time. I don't mean only when you're standing up; strain occurs as well when you work close to the ground with your back rounded for too long, or when you actually work on the ground, stretching and reaching too far for too long in any direction.

To keep your back from protesting while you garden, it's important that you occasionally stop to give it a break (well, not a "break," a good stretching out). One way to do this is to stand up with your feet slightly apart, hands placed in the small of your back, your fingertips pointing down for support. With your knees slightly flexed, gently press your chest forward to lift your breastbone upward just a bit.

If you do this motion correctly, you should experience a welcome stretch in your lower back. There's no need to take this motion to an extreme arch of your back. In fact, it's not recommended; excessive hyperextension (overarching) of the spine can compress the lumbar disks. Just hold the stretch for about eight to ten seconds while breathing naturally and comfortably.

How else do I relax my back? When taking a break to run into the house to make a phone call or grab a snack, I do an exercise that my friend Debbie taught me when I first began to garden years ago. For this stretch, you need a door frame. Stand in the door frame with your toes about twelve inches back from the floor line. Hold on to the frame at about shoulder height and lean back slightly to extend your arms. Make sure that you grasp the door frame with your thumbs down (no dirty gloves, please!) so that your fingers wrap the frame to support your weight when you pull back. Bend your knees as though you are about to sit down, keeping your rib cage and your pelvis vertical, one directly above the other. That's just the starting position.

Now for the stretch: Pretend someone has pushed a big rubber ball into your belly. The stretch happens when you pull back, tucking your buttocks under and rounding your back slightly. You then hold the position as long as necessary to release the tightness in your lower back. For me, it takes as little as thirty seconds, after which I'm ready to return to the garden with a back that's ready, willing, and able to take on more work.

Another soothing stretch I do for my garden-weary back is the cat stretch. You might be familiar with this back-soothing movement, perhaps from an exercise or yoga class, but never considered doing it in the garden. Why not? You're already on your hands and knees for much of your work anyway! It's just a matter of staying there, pulling in your belly and rounding your back, not unlike a cat's long, slow stretch after a nap. Just make certain that you lower your head and tuck your chin into your chest so there's no strain whatsoever on your neck.

To stretch your lower back still more, you can go directly from the cat stretch into a follow-up stretch by lowering your buttocks until they rest on or near your heels. Keep your head low and arms stretched in front. This two-part back-relieving stretch is one of my favorites, particularly after I've been weeding for too long on my hands and knees.

One of the first perennial beds I dug borders our little brook on the hill behind our house. When I planned and planted it, it never occurred to me that a garden bed on a hill could pose any problems whatsoever. However, every time I drag the hose or push the filled cart uphill to the bed, I question my sanity. Of course, at the time, I thought it was a brilliant idea to be able to stand at my kitchen sink and look out the window on a riot of midsummer color. And, indeed, my hilltop garden is really quite lovely to gaze at, that is, when the deer haven't turned it into a salad bar.

Before I even begin to work on the bed (having dragged, pulled, or pushed whatever up the hill), I give my upper back a brief massage by doing a few backward shoulder rolls. I do this by slowly lifting my shoulders up, pressing them back, down, and finally forward. This easy movement, which I repeat several times, is one of my standbys for relieving tightness in the shoulder area.

Besides shoulder rotations, I also do slow shoulder shrugs, which gently but effectively stretch the trapezius and rhomboid muscles located in the back of the neck and upper part of the back. To do the shrugs correctly, you slowly raise your shoulders toward your ears as far as you can without straining (you can do this while standing or seated). The upward movement should take

▼

about five seconds, so don't rush through it. Then let your shoulders slowly lower to their neutral position. Do three or four shrugs, making sure that you relax completely between each repetition, and bingo, the tightness is gone.

Another stretch for relaxing the upper back (I stop to do this when I'm turning the compost) is the following: With your feet comfortably apart and your hands resting on your waist, slowly press your elbows back bringing them as close together behind you as you can without straining. If you do this simple movement correctly and slowly, you will feel a pleasing stretch between your shoulder blades and across your chest. Again, it only takes a few repetitions.

To relax shoulder and upper back muscles that tire when you dig for too long, particularly when the ground is hard and dry, put your tool down and place the tips of your fingers on your shoulders, right hand on right shoulder, left hand on

left. Keeping your hands in place, slowly bring your elbows together at shoulder level, trying to touch them in front of your chin. A slow closing and opening motion, repeated several times, does wonders for relieving fatigue in the upper back.

One chore I must take short breaks from (I also dread doing it) is winding in the hose at the end of the day. Reeling it in (why is it invariably a tangled mess?) can be tiring, particularly on the upper back and shoulders, not to mention the operative arm.

Because some of my garden beds are somewhat far from the house (on the hill) and because we do not have an irrigation system, by day's end the long green monster is generally stretched to its utmost length. After lugging and tugging it down the hill or across the yard, I have to wind it up. (Of course, I could leave it out overnight, sprawled across the lawn like some of my less meticulous, well-adjusted friends do, but I don't!)

To minimize the discomfort that results from winding in what seems to be never-ending footage, I do a simple stretch that works in *opposition* to the forward arm and shoulder rotation. I stand up from my usual squatting position (it's a good idea not to squat for too long anyway) and place my fingers on my shoulders with my elbows extended out to the sides. I then form big, exaggerated backward circles with the elbows, which feels really good right between the shoulder blades. After four or five slow backward rotations, I'm ready and able (if not totally willing) to squat down and continue my hose retrieval.

In Hillsdale, we have an abundance of pine trees on our property, particularly behind the house. This is a plus during the winter months, for they create a veritable fairyland when laden with snow. But come fall, because I don't want the needles to remain on the lawn all winter (I'm too tidy and they're too acidic), I seduce Stephen into raking them up. The seduction goes as follows: For every hour he rakes, he earns a half-hour massage, redeemable that evening from the live-in masseuse.

Raking pine needles, like raking leaves, is tedious work that requires shoulder, upper back, and arm strength. Plus, there's all that bend-

ing over to put the needles into the cart, unless of course you drag them on a tarp to a disposal site (see page 56). Now, mind you, Stephen is in good shape (not necessarily from working in the garden!), but after thirty minutes or so of raking, he's ready for a time-out.

So he *temporarily* stops raking, and upon the advice of his personal trainer (aka wife), he does the following stretch to ease fatigue in his arms and shoulders. With his hands interlaced behind him, he slides them up his back and holds the lifted position for a few seconds. After repeating this simple stretch a few times, he's ready to take the rake in hand again.

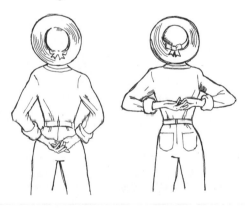

Another raking relaxer I recommend is done by placing your right hand on your left shoulder, with your elbow raised at approximately shoulder level. Using the heel of the left hand, you pull the right elbow slowly across your chest toward the left shoulder, keeping the elbow

parallel to the ground. You hold the stretch for about five seconds before you repeat it on the other side. This therapeutic stretch relieves upper arm and shoulder fatigue that results not only from raking but from hoeing as well.

"For it seems that proper gardeners never sit in their gardens. Dedicated and single-minded, the garden draws them into its embrace where their passions are never assuaged unless they are on their knees."

MIRABEL OSLER

FOR YOUR NECK

We don't often realize that we're overusing our neck muscles, or tensing them unnecessarily, until we end up with a pain in the neck. This can be avoided by working less intensely (particularly when pulling out defiant weeds) and also by occasion-ally moving your head out of a fixed position. Occasionally turning your head from side to side will keep neck stiffness at bay.

Here's an example: Last summer I decided to weed out each and every piece of goldenrod that had invaded my lupine border in front of the house by the road. Yanking these stubborn, deep-rooted fellows out was tough and tiring. Because I was somewhat rushed (not to mention hostile), I probably worked too quickly and too vigorously. The following morning, I woke up with a stiff neck, the result of unknowingly tensing my neck muscles while I weeded.

And that's just my point: While you work at any chore, particularly one that requires exertion, don't strain your neck by working too intensely. Ease up a bit. Even turning the head slowly from side to side (look over your shoulder) can keep neck muscles from becoming stiff and sore.

Neck discomfort can also occur if you're doing something that involves keeping your chin raised (and your head cocked back) for too long. This might occur when you prune the upper branches of a shrub or the lower branches of a tree.

To avoid stressing your neck muscles (particularly important if you suffer from arthritis in the neck), periodically stop and do the

▼

following stretch: Lower your chin toward your chest, stopping when you feel very slight tension on the back of your neck. Hold that position (but not your breath) until the tension begins to ease. Then lower your chin a bit farther, again stopping when you feel a slight stretch. Basically, you're making a double chin, which releases tightness in the muscles that run down the back of the neck.

For an equally effective stretch to keep neck muscles relaxed, which should be done as soon as you feel tension developing, place one hand on the back part of the top of the head. Then gently but continuously pull your head down (the shape of the stretch is like an upside-down J) until you feel the stretch all along the muscles of the back of your neck, especially up into the lower part of the back of your head.

The head roll is another simple exercise that prevents neck strain, and it's a cinch to do and takes no time at all. But one note of caution: Do not make a full circle with your head because dropping your head backward can harm the disks in your spine. This is important to keep in mind when you're pruning overhead branches or doing anything with your chin raised.

To practice the head roll the safe and correct way, slowly roll your left ear toward your left shoulder. Then lower your chin toward the ground keeping it tucked so that your neck vertebrae are as vertical as possible. Then roll your right ear toward your right shoulder. In essence, the movement pathway is side-center-side-center. This rolling motion should be done in a rhythmic, slow manner. No jerky moves for the neck, please! Since the head roll is such a basic and simple movement to weave into your work, you can manage it anytime, whether you're standing up or working on the ground.

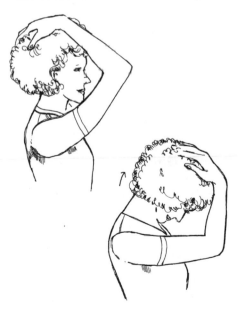

▼

"Being happy is dirt under your fingernails, wearing old clothes, having a good idea get better the longer you work at it, starting a new bed, giving plants away, and listening to rain."

GEOFFREY B. CHARLESWORTH

▲

FOR YOUR HANDS AND FINGERS

Your hands and fingers deserve some special time-out attention, too. Just think about it. When you're weeding, for instance, you continue to make a tight, fistlike, clenching motion that eventually tires and taxes the hands and fingers, no matter how protective your gloves might be.

This fist-making motion can become particularly difficult and painful if you suffer from arthritis in your fingers. To get some hand and finger relief, periodically stop what you're doing, remove your gloves, and move your fingers for a minute or two, just to stretch them out.

For example, separate them as much as you can, keeping them as straight as possible, until you feel a slight stretching tension. Or, with your fingers widely spread apart, you can make circles with your thumbs, first in one direction, then in reverse. Also, with your fingers apart, you can touch your thumb to each finger to relax the tendons in the palm of your hand.

On the subject of thumbs, if you do suffer from arthritis in your hands, be particularly careful of your thumb since it is a vulnerable joint. Try not to overwork or abuse it, for instance, by leaning on it while working on your hands and knees.

Another exercise I like to do, particularly if my hand tires from digging too long with a trowel, is a simple circular movement. Keep the wrist floppy and limp. Do several rotations, first in an outward direction, then inward. Then give your hand a good shaking out, which revs up circulation and feels wonderful.

If your hands begin to tire because of any repetitive motion, don't wait until fatigue turns into pain. Stop what you're doing as soon as you get the first distress signals so that you don't invite a more serious hand problem, such as carpal tunnel syndrome (see page 28). Naturally, when you are giving your hands a time-out stretch, you should remove your gloves so your hands can enjoy the full range of movement and get a well-deserved breath of fresh garden air.

"Soon her fingers were deftly pulling out tufts of grass and violets from around the bleeding heart; nothing like weeding to unknot the mind."

MAY SARTON

Time-Out

TO OXYGENATE

Speaking of fresh air, taking a brief time-out for some deep breathing sure has more than one advantage. Not only will it refresh and revitalize you, but conscious deep breathing also increases your awareness of scents and fragrances that can easily go unnoticed when you concentrate too intensely on your chores. A few deep breaths also tend to slow you down, which is good for your mind as well as your muscles.

While there are many different deep-breathing techniques, one easy and most effective way is while you're sitting on the ground, on a bench, in a chair, or, if you prefer, lying on your back under a big shade tree. This breathing technique has three parts that incorporate your abdominal, intercostal (chest), and clavicular (collarbone) areas; however, it's done in one continuous flow

Begin each breath by filling your abdomen, then expanding your chest, and finally raising your clavicle just slightly. You want to inhale through your nose because your nose, not your mouth, has a filter system, that is, the hair in your nostrils. By starting the breathing deep in your abdominal area (it will rise and descend fully and gently with the in-and-out cycle), your lungs have more room to expand, allowing a larger amount of air to enter.

As you inhale through your nose, you will notice that your abdomen expands as though it were being inflated with air. Only then do you allow the further expansion of your chest, which causes your rib cage to expand. Once the air rises to your chest, let it continue up to the top of your lungs. This will cause your collarbone to rise ever so slightly. By breathing this way, you will have filled your lungs from the bottom to the top with clean, fresh, delicious garden air.

Then what? Naturally, you have to exhale. This can be done either through the nose or the mouth. My preference is through the mouth since I'm better able to prolong the exhalation. When exhaling through your mouth, try to make a steady, extended note, such as *humm,* as in "hummingbird." Try as well to prolong the exhalation so that it is, ideally, twice as long as the inhalation.

That's all there is to it. You don't have to take lots of time out for this simple deep breathing, just enough to slow you down so you can smell the roses. While you breathe, take note of any tension or tightness in your neck, shoulders, lower back, or elsewhere. Simply being aware of any tension or tightness will help to breathe it away. You might want to give this breathing exercise a try right now.

Another equally effective breathing technique is done by first exhaling through the mouth, making an audible *whoosh* sound. You then close your mouth lightly, without tensing your lips, and slowly inhale through your nose quietly to the count of four. Once you have done so, you hold your breath for the count of four before exhaling through your mouth to the count of eight.

With both techniques, you want to achieve an exhalation that is twice as long as the inhalation, because you actually deepen respiration by exhaling more air, not inhaling it. When you push more air out of your lungs, your lungs automatically take more in. That's all there is to this simple drill. After four or five full breath cycles, just breathe normally and let yourself experience how your body feels. My guess is you'll feel more relaxed and refreshed. Give it a try.

"Everything that slows us down and forces patience, everything that sets us back into the slow cycles of nature, is help. Gardening is an instrument of grace."

MAY SARTON

TO HYDRATE

Like your plants and flowers, your body also needs water or it too will wilt. Gardening should absolutely drive you to drink—lots and lots of water, that is, even if you don't feel thirsty. Drinking water (which makes up 50 to 60 percent of your body) can enhance your energy. Particularly when the temperature is high and you perspire more profusely, be sure to stop at regular intervals for a water break. Remember, too,

thirst is satisfied long before you have replenished lost fluids. So hydrate, hydrate, hydrate!

When I head for the garden, it's never without my water bottle filled with cold "lemon water." We happen to be fortunate that our water not only tastes pure but tests pure as well. Nevertheless, I'm not a water drinker by nature, so I have to gussie it up a bit. I add a few ice cubes to the water (cooler drinks are absorbed more quickly than lukewarm ones) and either a few hefty squirts of fresh lemon juice or some fresh mint leaves—or both.

Though mint can be quite invasive, if you can spare the garden space, it's a must. It's easy to grow (tolerates sun or shade), looks and smells great in bouquets, can replace basil in a cooling pesto, and gives a clean, refreshing taste to water. Flavoring plain water with spearmint, apple mint, or peppermint leaves can make it far easier to swallow, so to speak.

I also find that putting water in a glass bottle instead of plastic is better because plastic can sometimes impart an undesirable taste to the water, particularly if the bottle sits out in the sun for hours.

But water need not be your only garden beverage. During the warmer months when I stop for an energy boosting snack, it's often in liquid form. There are many delicious, healthy drinks that you can whip up in the blender in no time and take with you into the garden, where you can sip while you snip and clip.

Or you can enjoy these refreshing drinks when you pop into the house for a break. They're cold, delicious, and just filling enough to stave off energy slumps. In fact, these quickie blender drinks (see recipes on p. 84) are ideal for enhancing energy when you feel too tired to toil or too pooped to plant. Because fruit and vegetable drinks provide a highly concentrated source of nutrients, they're an ideal snack before or after gardening. The only tools you need are a knife and blender.

Basically, these garden cocktails involve washing and cutting the fruit or vegetables; in some cases, adding a binder such as juice, yogurt, milk, or sorbet; and blending with or without ice. Here are a few tips for making these simple but delicious energy-boosting drinks.

▸ To keep calories low, opt for un-sweetened fresh or frozen fruit. (Frozen fruit will make a thicker drink.)

▸ To make frozen fruit, spread diced pieces on a cookie sheet and freeze for two to four hours; transfer the pieces to a resealable bag when hard. (Most supermarkets carry frozen, unsweetened strawberries, blueberries, raspberries, and other fruits.)

▸ For the creamiest, smoothest cocktail, let the ice sit at room temperature for ten to fifteen min-utes before blending. Also, the smaller the ice cubes, the better your blender can handle them. Fill trays only halfway or set the automatic ice maker to the small-est setting.

▸ Be daring and experimental. Try canned fruit nectars, such as guava, pear, apricot, or peach instead of juices; use tofu instead of yogurt, buttermilk instead of low-fat milk. Flavor with vanilla extract, freshly grated ginger, chopped fresh mint, or grated cit-rus peel.

To boost the health power of these cocktails, I often add soy. One ounce of soy protein (sold at natural food stores) will thicken your drink and add twenty grams of protein, less than one gram of fat, and a mere 100 calories to your drink.

You can also turn your fruit-filled cocktails into luscious frozen desserts to slowly savor while you work at your chores. To do this, just pour the contents into a glass bowl and cover. Freeze for about one hour, or until the mixture is thick-ened but not frozen, stirring several times in between. Now, the only tool you need is a spoon.

A final note of advice: Be sure that all fruits and vegetables used in your cocktails are thoroughly

Very Berry Banana Cocktail

2 cups low-fat milk
1 ripe banana, quartered
1 cup sliced fresh strawberries (or
    unsweetened frozen strawberries)
1 cup mixed fresh berries, such as
    raspberries, blueberries, and/or
    blackberries (or unsweetened
    frozen mixed berries)
Puree in a blender.
Serves 2–3

Minted Melon Cocktail

2 cups cantaloupe or honeydew melon,
    peeled and cubed
$1/4$ cup low-fat milk
3 teaspoons fresh mint, chopped
1 (8-ounce) carton vanilla fat-free
    yogurt

1. Place melon cubes in a single
   layer on a jelly-roll pan. Freeze
   cubes for 2 hours.
2. Place frozen melon and remaining
   ingredients in a blender, and
   process until mixture is smooth.
Serves 2

Melon Smoothie

2 cups cantaloupe, diced
1 cup honeydew melon, diced
1 cup seedless watermelon, diced
$1/2$ cup mango juice
1 tablespoon lime juice
10 large mint leaves
4 ice cubes

Combine all ingredients in the
blender, and whip until smooth.
Serves 2

Tropical Bliss

1 medium papaya
2 medium peaches
1 medium mango
3 ice cubes

1. Peel and pit fruit. Cut into
   chunks.
2. Blend until smooth.
Serves 2

Kiwi-Pineapple Cooler

1 cup fresh pineapple, cubed
$1/3$ cup pineapple juice
1 banana, quartered
4 ice cubes
4 kiwi, peeled and cubed

Place first four ingredients in a
blender; process until smooth. Add
kiwi, and process just until blended.
(Crushed kiwi seeds can taste bitter
so avoid overprocessing it.)
Serves 2

Tropical Dream

2 cups papaya, peeled and chopped
1 cup mango, peeled and chopped
$3/4$ cup pear nectar
1 tablespoon fresh lime or lemon juice
    (or both)

Place papaya and mango in a single
layer on a jelly-roll pan. Freeze at
least 1 hour. Place frozen fruit, nectar, and lime juice in a blender;
process until smooth.
Serves 2

▼

scrubbed before blending. This applies as well to any that may be peeled or have a rind, because slicing can transfer germs to the flesh of the fruit.

There's yet another blender recipe for a cooling, highly nutritious snack that I enjoy all summer long; for this one, you need vegetables—and a spoon. It's an easy-to-make, no-frills gazpacho—a real quickie that's healthy and delicious.

What else do I do to fortify myself while I work in the garden? Besides the Nutri-Power High Energy Bars, which I order by the boxful (they don't melt like Hershey Bars), I try,

for the most part, to keep my snacks healthy, natural, and energizing. Here are some of my standbys: bananas (they're easy to eat and digest); carrot sticks; Granny Smith apples; Pavich organically grown, jumbo raisins (they're the best); Wasa Crispbread (it's all natural, fat free and cholesterol free); and Paul Newman's Pretzels (I can't resist them). And I drink lots of lemon water, the colder the better to cool off fast.

Speaking of lemons, here's a luscious recipe for a cooling lemonade from a citrus-loving gardening friend.

Garden Variety Gazpacho

1 1/2 cups V8 or tomato juice (I prefer V8)

1 large carrot, peeled and cut into medium-size pieces

1 medium cucumber, peeled, seeded, and coarsely chopped

1 each green, red, and yellow pepper, cored, seeded, and coarsely chopped

pinch of cayenne pepper

freshly ground black pepper to taste

1 teaspoon medium-hot salsa

1. Wash and prepare the vegetables.
2. Blend all the ingredients until almost but not quite smooth.
3. Add a squirt of fresh lemon juice and top with chopped chives or fresh dill. To reduce the salt, you can substitute low sodium V8.

Serves 2

Linda's Lemonade

1/4 cup water

3/4 teaspoon sugar

1 cup lemon sorbet

3 teaspoons grated lemon rind

1/3 cup fresh lemon juice

10 ice cubes

1. Bring water and sugar to a boil in a small saucepan, stirring until sugar dissolves. Pour into a small bowl, cover, and chill.
2. Placed chilled sugar water, sorbet, and remaining ingredients in a blender; process until smooth. Sprinkle with fresh mint.

Serves 2

▽

"To dwell is to garden." ·
    MARTIN HEIDEGGER

△

TO MEDITATE

My garden is not only a welcomed place to work in but a welcomed space to rest and lull in as well. There, I can sit or stroll quietly. Without sounding like a flower child from the sixties, I can't imagine a better place for meditation than in a garden.

Ideally, meditating should help you let go of the buzzing thoughts cascading in your mind and bring you greater clarity and focus. Now, that may not always be the outcome for me, but if I sit still and just gaze at a beautiful flower or focus on a calming sound, such as the faint call of the chickadees in the pines, my internal clock slows down and I feel serene and content. So when anyone asks me, "What's the very best way to meditate?" My answer is, "Comfortably and quietly, in a garden."

To make the most of a garden meditation, ideally, you should find a spot where you can hide out and "chill out," even if it's for a mere five minutes. As you sit there, you might, as I do, focus on a particular flower or plant, or on a sound that's both pleasing and calming. One of my favorite spots is a tree stump near the brook. I can sit quietly there and listen to the water as it gently washes over the rocks. Or I might just focus on the sensation of the air as it enters and leaves my nostrils.

While you sit in your quiet spot, it's perfectly okay to praise yourself (and you should) for having created the beauty that surrounds you and for managing your life in a way that allows for times when you can just sit still and relish it all.

There are times when I prefer a strolling meditation, rather than sitting still. It's another way to bring harmony into my life and into my garden. To do this moving meditation, begin by standing still and taking a few deep, relaxing breaths, filling your lungs from bottom to top. You want to stroll around the garden, so find a pace that's slower than usual. As you move, be aware of your breath, but don't try to control it; you will find a comfortable rhythm between your breathing and your steps.

Bring your awareness to your senses, one at a time. Begin with your eyes: Look at all that surrounds you almost as if you were viewing your garden for the very first time. As you stroll, take note of the colors, textures, and shapes. Allow yourself to fully feel the pleasures derived from the sights that surround you.

Next, bring your awareness to your sense of smell. You might detect the delicate florals, the pungent smell of pine or herbs, or perhaps the rich smell of the soil

▼

beneath your feet. Give yourself time to take in all of nature's varied scents.

Then let your ears welcome all the sounds as if you were hearing them for the very first time. Your garden offers a rich symphony: birdcalls, insects buzzing, the rustling of leaves in the breeze, or perhaps water flowing in a brook or trickling from a fountain. Permit the sounds to wash over you as you continue to stroll.

Finally, turn your awareness to the sense of touch, not only by feeling an occasional petal or leaf, but by feeling the breeze or sun on your skin or feeling your muscles relax more and more. At the end of your stroll, blend all your sensory awareness and just experience being in your garden—in the present moment.

▼

"Flowers are restful to look at. They have neither emotions nor conflicts."

SIGMUND FREUD

▲

FOUR
▼▼▼▼▼

Cool Down and Clean Off

Gardening, like any rigorous sport or activity, should also be followed by a brief cool-down, even when the weather is cool. Since your back is the area that's really put to the test (all that lugging and tugging), it deserves a bit of extra pampering when you come in at the end of the day.

Once my chores are finished, before I even head for the tub or shower, I strip out of my dirty clothes and get down on the floor (on a rug or carpet) to "rock" and "roll" my knees. This two-part therapeutic sequence really feels good on my back and takes almost no time to do.

For the knee rock, bring both knees up to your chest with your hands placed just below the knees (or behind your knees), then slowly rock your knees toward your shoulders while keeping your abdominals pulled in. You should feel a good, comfortable stretch in the small of your back as you draw your knees

toward your body. Do this movement just until your back muscles relax.

Follow the "rock" with a "roll," which is a variation of the back extensor exercise on page 9. While still lying on your back with your knees bent, hook your left foot behind the right and extend your arms at shoulder level, palms down. Slowly lower both knees to the right (let the left knee lean on the right) until you feel the stretch across your

lower back. By allowing your head to roll in the opposite direction of your knees, you will experience the stretch even more.

But don't strain to lower your knees all the way. They need not touch the floor; go only as far as you can manage comfortably. You want to hold the stretch for four or five counts before bringing your knees back up to the starting position. Then, naturally, you do the same stretch to the left side, hooking the right foot behind the left. Keep alternating sides until your back muscles feel comfortably stretched. That's all there is to this mini-cool-down, at least on dry land. When you take a bath or shower, you can stretch your back muscles still more if you wish.

After hours in the garden, poking around in the soil, I can't imagine anything more appealing (short of a terrific massage, that is) than soaking in a warm, herb-scented bath while sipping a hydrating, cool glass of herbal tea. I mean, what could be more tempting than submerging yourself in a tub and·just lying there

feeling wonderfully clean, lazy, and luxurious after a day of heavy-duty gardening?

The sensation of soaking, with nothing between your skin and the caressing water, is not only soothing for the mind but for your garden-weary muscles and joints as well. From the moment your body touches the water, there's an instant sense of being nurtured. A soak in the tub can be particularly therapeutic when it's scented with your favorite herbs or flowers. Using plant oils, fragrances, and natural products to wash away a day's worth of garden grime is really a pleasant way to bring the garden right into your bathroom.

If you're like me, on workday mornings (and I don't mean working-in-the-garden mornings), most of the time, all you can do is pop in and out of the tub, settling for a quick once-over sudsing, or a short shower on the run. But when I finish gardening for the day, and my body not only needs cleansing but some pampering as well, there's nothing quite like a serene soak. Granted, if your only motive is to de-grime, a shower is much faster and efficient, but as restful and luxurious?—no way!

The water of the bath can be truly restorative. Tub time can also set the scene for the transition between gardening and the rest of your day. For me, bathing is a way to make an appointment with myself. It's that special time after I garden when I can retreat to yet another quiet place and treat myself kindly. A soothing, unhurried bath also allows me time to just lie back and contemplate all that I accomplished in the garden that day and, of course, to dream up all sorts of new plans and projects.

Although my bathroom in Hillsdale is hardly palatial, I create my private, little spa with the likes of soft lighting, a scented candle (rosemary is wonderful), soothing music (from my bedroom), as well as a variety of small ferns (they love the mistiness) planted in pretty cache pots. Then what?

While relaxing and soaking in the water, without detracting from the enjoyment of your bath, you can actually do some muscle-relaxing stretches. Just as the steamy heat from bath water opens pores, making them more receptive to skin softeners and cleansers, heat and humidity relax overworked muscles, increasing their stretch and contract capabilities.

You don't need an Olympic-size tub to do these after-gardening relaxercises. A standard one will do just fine. The magic ingredient is water. To create the most skin-loving, muscle-relaxing bath, you should keep the water between ninety and ninety-five degrees (roughly, body temperature).

If your bath is too hot, you run the risk of damaging your skin and of dilating capillaries. Very hot water can rob your skin of its natural oils, leaving it dry and tight. (If you have to hop up and down to keep from scalding your feet when getting into the tub, the water is too hot for sure.) A really hot bath also tends to be draining and debilitating making you feel sluggish and tired when you emerge instead of luxurious and refreshed.

The right temperature, on the other hand, will draw the blood gently to the surface to oxygenate the skin and carry away any toxins hiding just under the surface. In addition, it will *gently* increase perspiration to help eliminate impurities from your system. Even though your bath might feel just too marvelous for words, you should refrain from soaking indefinitely; limit your time to about fifteen minutes, twenty at most. Your skin is highly permeable and sensitive when it's wet and warm, so the effect of a fifteen-minute immersion can be truly dramatic.

Tub Stretches

FOR YOUR HANDS

Hands down, there's nothing quite like warm water for easing discomfort in the finger joints, often the result of planting bushels of bulbs or weeding for too many hours. As a matter of fact, if you suffer from arthritic fingers, *before* you work in the garden, submerge your hands in a basin or sink of warm water for a few minutes to loosen and limber them up. While they're submerged, you can actually do the same hand-limbering exercises that I recommend for the tub.

For starters, walk your fingers on the tub floor, beginning with the thumb and working to the pinky, then go in reverse. Press down moderately so you feel the stretch but not with so much effort that you strain your finger joints. Always exercise both hands, even if only one feels sore or painful.

With your hands underwater, you can also roll them from the wrist, first in a clockwise direction, then counterclockwise, not unlike the exercise I suggested that you do in the garden to relieve hand fatigue from weeding. After a few rotations with each hand, lift them out of the water and just shake them gently to rev up the circulation.

Or, with your hands underwater, make tight fists, then open your hands wide to stretch the fingers. If, however, you suffer from arthritis in your fingers, be careful not to make too rigid a clenching motion; keep it gentle. This holds true as well for when you work in the garden; avoid clenching or gripping your hand with too much intensity, whether around a weed, a tool, the hose handle, or whatever.

You can also bring relief to tired finger joints by massaging your hands while they're submerged. If you add a few drops of your favorite massage oil to the water, not only will it facilitate the massaging action but it will also soothe your hands and fingers.

To massage your hands, keep one hand submerged and use the thumb of the other hand to do the work. Begin by pressing your thumb into your palm and forming a clockwise circle. Exert enough pressure to feel the massage, but not so much that you experience any pain. Make the circles on various spots of the palm, starting at the base of the pinky and working to the base of the thumb, then finally around to the heel of the hand. In essence, you move in a circular direction all around the palm. Once you have completed this brief hand massage, bend each finger back just slightly, using pressure from the thumb of the other hand and keeping your hand under the water the entire time.

FOR YOUR SHOULDERS

Tired shoulder muscles can also be pampered while you sit and soak in the tub. Even if you do not submerge them entirely, the heat from the bath water will relax your shoulder muscles as you gently stretch and massage them. The easy shoulder soothers listed below really feel good after you've raked far more leaves than planned.

For starters, roll your shoulders back slowly several times, either simultaneously or one at a time (just as I suggested you do in the garden). You can also shrug them slowly up and down (another in-the-garden stretch). These two simple motions not only ease shoulder tightness but relax the neck muscles as well.

"Don't wear perfume in the garden, unless you want to be pollinated by bees."

ANNE RAVER

In addition to these very basic movements that relax the shoulder area, you can also massage your shoulders while you soak. Begin by making a fist (but don't clench too tightly) with your right hand. Keeping your wrist loose, gently pound your left shoulder. Next, lightly tap the side of your neck, then work across your chest and back to the top of your left shoulder. When you're finished, switch sides and do the same on your right shoulder.

Another way to massage the shoulders is to curve your fingers on both hands and place them over the tops of your shoulders, right hand on right shoulder, left hand on left. You then press the tightest spot on

your shoulder with your index, middle, and ring fingers. Allow the weight of your arms to relax forward, with your fingers hooked onto the shoulder tension. Breathe deeply while you maintain finger-hooking

pressure for about one minute.

Next, feel for another tense spot on your shoulders. (This should be near the one you just worked on. Just move your hands along, between your neck and the end of your shoulder.) Once you find the spot, gradually apply firm pressure directly on your shoulder tension again. Let your arms relax forward, keeping your fingers curved like a hook. Allow your fingers to sink deeper into the muscles as they soften and relax. Hold for one minute as you take slow, deep breaths. Then lower your hands and let them relax under the water before you give them a good shaking out.

FOR YOUR LEGS AND FEET

What else can you do while you soak to relax your garden-weary muscles? For one thing, you can relieve overworked, tight calf muscles that result, for instance, from using an edger on hard, rocky soil. For this calf relaxer, extend your legs in front so that the soles of your feet are pressed against the end of the tub. Then flex your feet (bring your toes up toward the ankles) as hard as you can and hold the flexed position for about twenty seconds. You should feel a gentle pull behind the legs, not only in the calves but behind the knees as well.

After you've done this stretch, let your legs go totally limp on the tub floor. Then, with your legs extended again, separate your feet and just roll them inward (pigeon-toed), then outward. Repeat several times. This rolling motion relaxes the entire leg from top to bottom; even your toes benefit.

Speaking of toes, just wiggling them under the water, or better yet, placing them under the faucet for a whirlpool effect, feels great after they've been stuffed into work shoes or boots all day.

FOR YOUR BACK

Tired back muscles can really benefit from stretching when they're submerged in warm water. Here's a simple stretch that works all the time. Begin by bending your knees (but not too much), then wrap your arms under your thighs. With your chin low and your back rounded (head above water, please), relax your neck and let your lower back and your neck stretch out for thirty to sixty seconds. This stretch

feels good on the lower and upper back.

Here's another stretch that eases garden-fatigued back muscles. Extend one leg forward and bring the other knee up toward your chest, with your hands resting just below the kneecap. For this exercise, you want to lean back against the tub so that you feel secure and comfortable. Hold the bent knee to your chest with both hands for about eight seconds before you change to the other leg. The closer your knee comes to your chest, the more stretch you will feel on the lower back. For additional comfort while doing this stretch, rest your back, as I do, against a small rubber bath pillow.

One note of caution: Because you might be adding oil to the bath water, to prevent slipping and sliding while doing these stretches, use a

▼

▽ ▽ ▽ ▽ ▽ **TIP** ▽ ▽ ▽ ▽ ▽

By infusing water with pine needles and witch hazel, you can make a cooling and slightly astringent lotion. This lotion not only refreshes your skin but stimulates circulation as well. Best of all, this homemade toner contains none of the alcohol, preservatives, or fragrances of store-bought products:

1 cup fresh (well-rinsed) pine needles
1 cup distilled water
1/4 cup witch hazel

Put the pine needles and water into a small saucepan. Bring to a boil, then remove pan from heat. Cool completely, then strain away the needles. Add witch hazel and stir well. Store in a clean glass bottle in a cool, dry place.

rubber tub mat. Use it when stretching in the shower as well.

Baths and Brews

A fragrant herbal bath seems the natural choice after I garden. In fact, rarely would I consider soaking in plain, ordinary water, not when the choices are so seductive—rosemary, eucalyptus, geranium, pine—the possibilities are endless. For me, floral and herbal fragrances can be extremely evocative, creating not only conscious but unconscious responses as well. The scent of roses, for instance, conjures loving and happy memories of my dear, diminutive Aunt Martha, who truly did smell like a rose.

But there's even more to the essence of the rose, according to experts. It supposedly stimulates receptors in the brain that can relieve sadness and can calm and soothe the nerves. Now, I don't know if that's really true; what I do know is that after soaking for just five minutes in a rose-scented bath, I become a very serene, contented lady.

One lovely and very appealing bath for after-gardening combines the fresh, alluring fragrance of rose with that of geranium. For this bath, I use oils that I purchase at Crabtree and Evelyn in New York City. In fact, the company produces several products especially for gardeners (available nationwide at Crabtree and Evelyn stores and some pharmacies), including a Hand Therapy Cream as well as vegetable-based Scrub Bars made from the likes of lettuce, cucumber, and carrot.

For my soothing geranium-and-rose soak, I combine eight or nine drops of rose oil and about four or five drops of geranium oil. I run the bath to a comfortable temperature, and when it's nearly full, I add the oils, first the rose, followed by the geranium. The scent of the latter intensifies the rose-rich water and perfumes the bathroom with a lovely fragrance.

Flower-infused waters make a naturally gentle facial freshener, so while I soak, I might blot my skin from time to time with a cotton ball moistened with rose water. This refreshing skin treatment from Kiehl's in Manhattan is cleansing and toning without being overly scented or too astringent.

There's no better time to apply moisturizer to your face and neck than while you soak or just after when your pores are receptive and drink it up. So, to add yet another touch of rose to this pampering bath, I apply Dr. Hauschka's Rose Skin Cream (it's one of my favorite moisturizers) to my face and neck. Dr. Hauschka offers a superb skin care line, available at health food stores or by mail order.

Speaking of roses, they're more than just a feast for the eyes or breakfast for the bees: Roses have been used medicinally for centuries. Fresh rose hips (the fruit of the plant) are highly nutritious. In fact, tea made from rose hips (which contain more vitamin C, ounce for ounce, than oranges) is healthy and hydrating and can be leisurely sipped while you soak in your rose-scented bath. (That's of course providing you do *not* spray your roses.) Rose hip tea can be enjoyed hot or, as I prefer, iced with a sprig of fresh mint.

To make this vitamin-rich tea, just grind up the hips (they also boast an ample supply of vitamin A) in a coffee grinder and steep one teaspoon of the grounds in a cup of very hot water for about ten minutes. I recommend very hot, not boiling, water because boiling water will decrease the tea's vitamin C content. If you like a sweeter brew, just add a bit of honey.

If rose hips are not your cup of tea, another infusion you can sip, hot or cold, while you soak is a tea made from lemon balm. According to Nicholas Culpeper, the seventeenth-century herbalist (who wrote his advice in English rather than Latin so that his recommendations could be followed more easily by the common people), "Lemon balm driveth away all troublesome care and thoughts out of the mind, arising from melancholy and black choler." Again, I'm not certain how accurate this theory is, but lemon balm tea is another brew I enjoy after I've gardened.

I've been growing lemon balm for many years, ever since a trip to the Cotswolds introduced me to this herb often found in English herb gardens. This simple to grow, lemon-scented plant thrives in poor soil and in partial shade and can be propagated from seed sown in spring or by dividing. Like mint, it

▼

▽ ▽ ▽ ▽ ▽ TIP ▽ ▽ ▽ ▽ ▽

Here's a pleasant herbal infusion that removes grime and dirt from your face without alcohol and preservatives. Stored in the refrigerator, this toner makes a refreshing warm-weather treatment when you pop into the house to take a break and give your face a cooling off. Add two tablespoons of dried chamomile flowers and one tablespoon of rosemary to a cup of boiling water. Steep it for twenty minutes, then strain away the herbs. Apply the toner to your face with a cotton ball, or use a spray bottle. It not only smells clean and refreshing but will give your face a natural lift. You can keep this delicately scented facial spritz for a week in the refrigerator.

flourishes with the least bit of care and attention. In fact, lemon balm is best planted where it's not too conspicuous because of its weedy habit: It can be quite invasive if you're too lenient with it.

According to Anne McIntyre's informative book *Flower Power* (Henry Holt), while enhancing relaxation, lemon balm is also very restorative. "It lifts the spirits, improves memory and helps tired brains to concentrate." (Not a bad trio!)

To make lemon balm tea, simply steep one quarter cup of fresh chopped leaves in one cup of boiling water for up to ten minutes. Not only is this citrus-scented drink soothing for frazzled nerves but for frazzled digestion too.

A note or two of caution regarding lemon balm: It has been shown to inhibit certain thyroid hormones. For this reason, people suffering from Graves' disease or other thyroid-related problems should use it only with a doctor's approval. What lemon balm certainly does *not* inhibit are bees; it's an excellent plant for attracting them to the garden, should that be your inclination.

While you sip your lemon balm tea, you could also be soaking in a lemon balm bath. To do this, just tie a handful of balm into a muslin bag and run your bath water over it. The combination of a lemon-flavored tea and a citrus-scented soak will set the scene for sweet dreams, I can assure you.

On the topic of sleep-inducing brews (not that you probably need one after a rigorous day of gardening), chamomile tea is effective for relaxing before bedtime, and delicious hot or iced. It also makes a pleasant-tasting brew to sip while you soak in the tub. Loved the world over, in the United States, chamomile (with its delicate yellow-and-white daisylike flower) ranks with the top-selling herbs, which is no wonder since chamomile is supposedly packed with medicinal benefits.

The medicinal power of chamomile comes from the volatile oil in the flower. When you prepare tea from your own crop (it likes well-drained soil in a sunny spot), keep in mind that boiling destroys the oil. You want to boil the water separately and then put it over the flowers to steep. To make tea, steep one to two teaspoons of pulverized dried flower heads in one cup of hot water for ten to fifteen minutes.

Here's something you might find useful: Not only does chamomile benefit ailing people but, according to McIntyre, it has also traditionally cured sick plants and was thus known as the "plants' physician." So the next time your flowers are pooped and droop in a vase, try adding some chamomile tea to the water to rev them up.

But let me mention one chamomile caution: Although considered one of the safest herbal remedies, it can cause an allergic reaction in pollen-sensitive individuals. If you happen to be allergic to ragweed, aster, or chrysanthemums, you may very well have a reaction to even one cup of chamomile tea, so you should be cautious about drinking it. Susceptible persons have reported hives, hay fever, and asthma.

Teas, such as the ones made from rose hips, lemon balm, and chamomile, can be a welcome, healthy alternative to caffeine-based beverages (soda and coffee), which you might otherwise drink while or after you garden. These herbal teas (which will not make you jumpy) can be enjoyed iced in summer or hot in winter. Although herbal tea brands continue to multiply and are readily available at stores, I think it's much more fun and satisfying to use herbs grown in your own garden.

As a rule, when brewing your own herbal teas (use a nonmetal pot), allow the tea to steep for ten to fifteen minutes, no longer, before straining and drinking it. Place the herbs in a warmed pot, measure and pour in the required amount of boiling water, and cover. Allow two level teaspoons of dried herbs or two level tablespoons of fresh herbs for each cup.

Don't increase the infusion time in the hope of intensifying the flavor. Prolonged exposure to heat causes a loss of volatile oils through evaporation. If a stronger infusion is desired, add more leaves, but don't steep too long, which can impart a bitter taste.

For sweetness, if desired, add a bit of honey or sugar, but refrain from adding milk since it will cloud the delicate color. If you wish to keep dried herbs for your teas and want to keep them for the winter, place them in opaque, airtight glass jars or containers to retain their flavor, much like ordinary teas.

Once you have enjoyed the benefits of homemade herbal teas, you may become your own tea designer. By mixing two or more types of aromatic leaves and flowers, you can create innumerable permutations of flavors while benefiting from the healing properties of more than one plant.

But one very important note of caution: Do not use flowers or herbs for your teas, or for any cooking for that matter, that have been sprayed or dusted with insect poisons. If you buy flowers or herbs from a commercial florist to make your own teas, be sure to ask if any sprays have been used on them and if those sprays were water-soluble. If the flowers were subjected to sprays that cannot be rinsed off with water, do not use *any* part of the plant for bathing or consumption.

But enough about what to sip while you soak; let's get back to what you soak in. If you grow your own lavender, you can use it for a muscle-relaxing soak. Simply fill a cotton or muslin bag with fresh lavender flowers and leaves (as you did for your lemon balm bath). Tie the bag so that you can hang it under the faucet. Then run warm water over it, squeezing the bag periodically to release the lavender oil.

Not only does lavender have a lovely, alluring scent, but this fragrant member of the mint family (yes, mint!) also soothes sunburn and discomfort from insect bites, which makes it all the more attractive and appealing for a bath after gardening.

Actually, lavender contains a long list of biologically active compounds, some proven to kill bacteria and viruses. Rumor has it that Roman soldiers carried it with them in their medical kits to use as a disinfectant, a practice that carried over into the Middle Ages. Even today, particularly in France where lavender is so very popular, the diluted oil, strong infusion, or tincture of lavender is dabbed on cuts, wounds, and sores as a disinfectant.

As for those very proper Victorian women, who we know were prone to swooning (because their corsets were too tight, not because they gardened too strenuously), they carried handkerchiefs scented with lavender oil or rubbed lavender oil onto their temples for stress relief.

Aēsop, a wonderful Australian

skin product line (no animal testing) sold at Barneys in Manhattan, features a lavender oil that I really like. This product combines lavender with peppermint and lemon, a unique blend. Not only do I use six to eight drops in the tub when I bathe, but I also rub several drops of oil on my still damp feet after a bath or shower. Hours after application, the delicate combination of scents continues to keep my feet smelling sweet and feeling smooth.

The other massage oil in the Aēsop line that I enjoy is the blend of frankincense, bergamot, and sandalwood. I apply it to my clean, slightly damp skin after I bathe, because, unlike many massage oils that have stained (and thus ruined) my clothing, Aēsop oils never leave any color or residue.

A few words of caution regarding the use of oils on your skin: Avoid applying them directly to your face. Even though they might be highly diluted in a bathtub of water, they are not recommended for delicate facial skin. Eye contact should be avoided as well. And if you're pregnant, there are many herbs, such as basil, cinnamon, sage, and rosemary, that you should avoid putting in your bath. So be sure your choice of herbs is safe before you take the plunge.

There's another bath oil I recommend. Though it might not smell as wonderful, it's truly therapeutic for

> ▿ ▿ ▿ ▿ ▿ **TIP** ▿ ▿ ▿ ▿ ▿
>
> Here's a time-saving nail trick: Massage hair conditioner into your cuticles while you shower, then push them gently back with the edge of a washcloth.

sore muscles and joints. This muscle-melting soak is one of my after-gardening standbys because it invariably brings quick relief, particularly when my back feels achy.

For this bath you need six to eight drops of camphor oil, which you can purchase at a pharmacy. In addition, you will need two cups of evaporated milk, which keeps your skin well-coated for the topical relief that results from the camphor oil. Run the bath water comfortably hot, and pour the evaporated milk near the tap so that the water disperses the creamy substance. When the bath is nearly full, add the camphor oil. Swirl the water vigorously to combine the oil thoroughly with the milk-enriched water.

As you soak there and breathe in the penetrating aroma, talk to your muscles and direct them to relax and go limp. To further urge them to let go, with your feet and your knees together, shift your knees from right to left from time to time. This simple motion, coupled with the heat and camphor, will bring still more relief to sore lower back muscles.

In fact, when my back really feels

overworked, after I soak in this therapeutic bath, I dry off and do the "rock" and "roll" stretches (page 89) that I recommended for after gardening. I do the stretches right on the hooked rug in my bedroom, and because my muscles are limp and relaxed from the moist heat and camphor, they respond particularly well and quickly.

"Won't you come into the garden? I would like my roses to see you."
RICHARD BRINSLEY SHERIDAN

Shower Soothers

I realize you might share my enthusiasm for gardening but not necessarily for bathing. In truth, soaking in stagnant water filled with garden grime doesn't appeal to me either. What I often do when I come in from the garden *really* dirty is take a quick shower first. Showering then soaking gives me the fullest possible cleansing plus relaxing results.

If you opt to shower instead of taking a bath, you can still do some muscle-soothing stretches while you stand to clean off. If you direct the water to the very spots that need relief, these shower soothers will work all the more.

Many of the time-out stretches that I recommended for the garden can be done in the shower as well.

The advantage of doing them with the aid of warm water, rather than on dry land, is that the moist heat will make your muscles even more receptive to stretching and relaxing. Naturally, for safety's sake, always stand on a rubber mat.

FOR YOUR NECK

Let's take it from the top. Start your shower by directing the water to the back of your head and neck. Then turn your head slowly from right to left (look over your shoulder). It's as easy as that.

Next, slowly lift and lower your chin, just a bit, several times, to ease any back of the neck tightness. But make certain, particularly if you suffer from arthritis in your neck, that you do not cock your head back too far (or drop it too far forward), which can exacerbate joint inflammation.

That's an important movement principle you should remember to apply when you garden as well. Although you do not want to keep your head in a rigid position while you work, by keeping it neutral (not too far forward or too far back), you will avoid stressing the neck joints and overworking the neck muscles.

The dorsal glide is also effective for relieving tight neck muscles. Again, you want the water to hit the back of your neck while you stand tall, looking straight ahead. Slowly tuck your chin as you glide your head backwards over your body. Try to hold the position for four counts before you relax into the neutral position. (This is a little weird looking, but it works!) The dorsal glide

can be done in the garden, too.

While the water hits the back of your head and neck, you can effectively massage that area by placing your thumbs underneath the base of your skull in the indentations that lie about two to three inches apart. Gradually press up under the skull for about thirty seconds.

Next, slide your thumbs outward to the indentations behind the lower edge of your earlobes. With your thumbs in place, gradually press and

hold, again for about thirty seconds. These points often become sore and sensitive, for instance, from stressing your neck when you lift or carry heavy garden supplies.

"You can't plough a field by turning it over in your mind."

ANONYMOUS

FOR YOUR UPPER BACK

Although I've called the lower back the gardener's prime "hot spot," the muscles in the upper back certainly get a workout, too, when you're lifting and lugging plant matter, tools, or whatever. You know the area I mean: right smack between your shoulder blades. To ease and relax those muscles, you want to direct the water to that very spot.

Begin by resting your hands on your shoulders, elbows straight out to the sides. (You might have to turn just slightly to avoid touching the wall with your elbow.) In this position, first form backward circles with

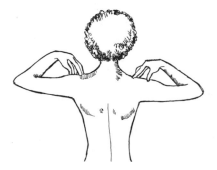

your elbows several times, then change direction and rotate them forward.

Another upper back relaxer can be done by clasping your hands behind your back and lifting your arms as high as you can without straining. Once they're raised, either hold them in the lifted position or you can gently push them upward several times before lowering them. This exercise gives the upper back, arms, and shoulder muscles a good de-kinking. In fact, I frequently stop to do this very stretch while raking

leaves in the fall.

FOR YOUR LOWER BACK

For your lower back, direct the water so that it targets your lumbar spine (just below your waist), the area that tends to protest the most from overexertion. This lower back relaxer really feels good when your

back doesn't feel so good. With your feet placed comfortably apart and secure on the mat, bend your knees, rest your palms on your thighs, and lean forward with your back as

straight and lengthened as possible.

You then move from the straight back position to a rounded back while exhaling your breath and pulling in your abdominal muscles. In this rounded position, your head should be lowered, chin tucked. Repeat the sequence of flat spine-rounded spine two or three times,

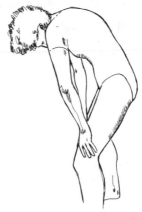

slowly and carefully, holding each position for two counts, before you straighten up completely. This is actually a variation of the cat stretch, which I suggested you do from time to time while you work on your hands and knees in the garden (see page 75). And it really does relax the lower back, particularly when the water hits you just where your back feels stiff or sore.

"Gardeners have certainly arisen by culture and not by natural selection. If they had developed naturally they would look differently; they would have legs like beetles, so that they need not sit on their heels, and they would have wings, in the first place for their beauty, and, secondly so that they might float over the beds."

KAREL ČAPEK

Body Care for Nails, Hands, Feet, and Face

LOOFAH MASSAGE

Using a loofah for after-gardening grime removal not only works well but feels good and benefits your skin and circulation. A loofah, in case you're not familiar with it, is the dried fibrous residue of the cucumber relative *Luffa cylindrica*. I personally prefer it to a washcloth because it does a far better job sloughing off dead skin and improving blood circulation. I buy my loofahs, in all shapes and sizes, either at a pharmacy or at a natural food store.

Here's how to use a loofah most effectively for both cleaning and circulation enhancement: First, you want to lather your entire body with soap or a bath gel. One of my favorite gels is Foaming Scrub from L'Occitane en Provence, the makers of an excellent line of bath and skin products. Made of plant microparticles, this particular gel not only removes dead skin but also softens rough skin, leaving it smooth and revitalized. L'Occitane products are sold at several New York locations as well as in New Jersey, Connecticut, and Washington, D.C.

Or instead of the gel, I might use Soap on a Rope, also from L'Occitane, either in honeysuckle or verbena. Although these soaps are, admittedly, a bit of an indulgence (far more costly than a bar of Ivory or Dove), they really are quite special and add pleasure (and fragrance) to after-gardening cleaning off.

After I lather my body with the loofah, I brush up the arms, then down the neck and shoulders to the back and stomach. I then start again at the toes, moving up the legs and over the thighs. In this way, I'm working toward the heart, an essential feature of good massage technique.

In addition to a loofah, you can

also use brushes made from sisal, which have a similar massaging effect. If you do use either loofahs or sisal products for after-gardening cleaning off, it's important that you clean them off as well. That means wash them out in warm then cold water to prevent them from degenerating too rapidly and becoming discolored.

"Unless you take care, the sun will pin you down. Put a hat on that foolish head of yours when you go out into the fields."

FARMER'S ALMANAC

NAILS AND HANDS

After a day in the garden, even if you do wear gloves for the majority of your chores, there's invariably some dirt and grime embedded under your fingernails. As I already noted, one way to keep under-the-nail dirt to a minimum is to run your fingers along a wet bar of soap before you go into the garden. When your chores are completed and you're cleaning off in the tub or shower, you can do this once again before using a nail brush.

For nail cleaning, the soap should be mildly abrasive to get the job done without causing peeling. Two soaps that work well for nail care and clean-up come from the Sun Feather Handcrafted Herbal Soap Company, a product line that was brought to my attention by a participant in one of my workshops. Sun Feather is a great soap source, and their products are cruelty-free. One of the soaps I particularly like is Gentleman Farmer's Soap, which contains ground corn and olive oil. The other is Worker's Soap, which blends spice oils with pumice bits and cocoa butter. Both soaps are sufficiently abrasive to get the job done.

When cleaning garden-dirty fingernails, avoid rubbing them with too much force; excessive rubbing can create brittle nails. Use a brush that has soft or fine bristles (you can even use a soft toothbrush) to minimize distress to the skin. Make certain not to file your nails after you soak in the tub unless they're bone dry. Filing wet nails can cause the fibers to separate, thus encouraging further splitting. To prevent nails from breaking while you garden, avoid filing deep into corners: By allowing your nails to grow along the sides, they will be stronger.

Once the nails are dry, you can then use an orangewood stick for extra cleansing. Just dip it in an astringent (such as diluted tea tree oil) and swipe around the entire cuticle. Since the cuticles are pliable after a bath or shower, you can then push them back *gently* without causing harm. If you have sensitive cuticles, as I do, use a cuticle pusher with a cushioned tip, which softens the pressure considerably. By gently pushing the cuticles back, the growth and health of your nails will be enhanced. Remember, however, excessive pushing of the nail matrix may cause damage, possibly inhibiting nail growth, so be careful.

You should also massage some cuticle cream onto each fingertip and nail base, waiting a few minutes until they're soft and saturated. One product that works really well for my nails is Kiehl's Moisturizing Cuticle Treatment, which is thick and very rich. The other is Farmer's Market Lemon Cuticle Cream by Burt's Bees, which I like for its consistency and citrus scent.

If and when my nails have to come out from under wraps (garden gloves) and make a public appearance, I might use a white pencil on the underside of the nail tip to give them a well-groomed look. For maneuverability, be sure to moisten the pencil tip so it glides easily under the nail. Buffing the nails also gives them a clean, healthy appearance.

Even if I wear gloves for the majority of my gardening chores, I avoid using bright-colored lacquers, which can chip and then look messy. Instead, I apply clear polish, which protects my nails and doesn't require constant touching-up. If you do wear clear polish, or any polish for that matter, avoid polishing to the

> ▽ ▽ ▽ ▽ ▽ **TIP** ▽ ▽ ▽ ▽ ▽
>
> Nail polish provides some UV protection, and a number of polishes now include sunscreen, so check the labels.

cuticle's edge. Lacquer can dry out cuticles, cracking them, which allows dirt to do its damage, particularly if you don't wear gloves.

After I bathe or shower, in addition to moisturizing my cuticles (almond and olive oil are also excellent nail and cuticle conditioners), I slather my hands with a heavy-duty hand cream from Kiehl's, a company that manufactures excellent products and has been in operation since 1851 (hardly newcomers to the skin care scene). The cream I use is unusually rich but not greasy, and it gets high marks from my friends who, like me, are always in search for the miracle product for garden-ravaged hands. (As a bonus, it is SPF 8.)

If gardening has left its mark on my hands in the form of cuts or nicks, after I shower or bathe, I slather on Farmer's Friend Hand Salve from Burt's Bees, available at garden centers nationwide. This highly protective, pleasant-smelling salve, made with botanical oils, herbs, beeswax, and the aromatic essence of flowers and leaves selected especially for their soothing qualities, really does work on hands that cry out for some tender loving care. It too is a favorite among my gardening pals.

In fact, many of the Burt's Bees all-natural products are ideal for gardeners, including their poison ivy soap, beeswax lip balm, and bug repellent, to name just a few. These, and other Farmer's Friend products from Burt's Bees, are offered through an excellent catalog (well worth the two dollars) from Well-Sweep Herb Farm. According to my friend Wendy, who gardens on Fire Island (talk about a deer problem!) and brought this catalog to my attention, the Well-Sweep farm, located between Hackettstown and Washington, New Jersey, is well worth a visit.

When my hands really look wrecked, before bedtime I might slather on Badger Healing Balm, Bag Balm (both sold at garden supply stores), or gobs of plain old Vaseline. Then I tuck my hands into thin, white While*U*Sleep Gloves (providing Stephen is out-of-town), which I purchase in large quantities at Rite-Aid. By morning, not only do my hands look better, they feel better, too.

Speaking of gloves, I discovered a useful item at the Body Shop in Manhattan, a "moisturizing" glove made from 88 percent cotton and 12 percent Lycra. These gloves have a cozy fit and allow my hands to move comfortably while my moisturizer does its magic, be it while I'm asleep or awake. (The gloves, along with a potent hand cream, make a perfect gift for a gardener on your Christmas list.)

"There is one thing that you will find practically impossible to carry into your own greenhouse and that is tension."

CHARLES H. POTTER

FOOT CARE

When time permits, another element I might include in my after-gardening pampering routine is a brief foot massage. Granted, your feet don't get abused the way your hands do when you toil in the soil, but planting them firmly on spades, shovels, or edgers can be tough on your tootsies.

A foot massage eases tension in the muscles and stimulates the blood supply to and around the feet. So here's the rub for a quick, do-it-yourself foot massage after you bathe or shower: In a small bowl, mix some unscented oil (I use Nivea Conditioning Oil) with two or three drops of oil of peppermint. The latter gives a cooling, refreshing result. Or instead of creating your own foot rub, you can buy a peppermint-based foot lotion, such as Peppermint Foot and Leg Lotion by

Dr. Scholl.

Peppermint's menthol acts as a counterirritant on your skin, causing a cooling sensation that relieves soreness and pain. (That's why menthol is included in many topical pain-relieving substances, such as muscle rubs and cough drops.) Because of peppermint's strength, you need very little essential oil for this foot-massaging treat(ment).

Because of its pungent taste and pleasing aroma, peppermint has been one of the best loved herbs ever since this hybrid was found sprouting among the spearmint bushes in England in the late seventeenth century. Since then, it has been added to everything from toothpaste to foot products. But remember, not all mints are created equal. If you purchase a peppermint product, whether it's a tea or a foot lotion, make sure the label specifies peppermint and not just mint. The mint family includes the flavorful spearmint, as well as lavender and rosemary, but only peppermint contains menthol, a foot-cooling remedy.

For this easy peppermint foot massage, place a terry cloth towel on a comfortable chair, or if you prefer, place the towel on the floor. Once you have mixed the lotion with the peppermint oil, apply it to one foot. Begin by massaging your toes, pulling each one gently, then rotating them one by one. Next, move up the foot toward the ankle, using your thumbs to massage around the ankle bones. Massage under the ball of the foot with the fingers of both hands, then up into the instep and finally to the heel and up into the ankle once again.

Next, hold the foot at the ankle with both hands so you can rotate the foot slowly, first in a clockwise direction several times, then in reverse. End by smoothly and continuously stroking both hands over the entire foot from toe to ankle, always going toward not away from the heart. You will notice how the blood is circulating, yet the skin will feel cooler from the peppermint. Repeat the same sequence on the other foot.

Another effective remedy for garden-weary, puffy feet is a sandalwood foot soak, which you can also enjoy after your bath or shower. For this soak, add a handful of fragrant sandalwood powder (available at natural food stores) to a basin of tepid water and let your tired tootsies relax for ten or fifteen minutes while you sit in a chair and read or simply close your eyes and rest.

FACE-LIFTS . . . NATURALLY

The best part of making your own skin treatments with fresh ingredients is that you avoid exposure to the additives that give shelf life to packaged products. Plus, it's fun sometimes to experiment with flowers, fruits, vegetables, and herbs that grow right in your garden.

At the urging of a client (who's not only an avid gardener but a naturalist when it comes to skin care), I've experimented with several homemade facial potions that cleanse and refresh the skin after a sweaty day in the garden.

Raw strawberries, for instance, are a natural cleanser and leave a sweet, lingering fragrance, while crushed almonds exfoliate. Add yogurt, cucumber, and eggs, which soothe and soften the skin, and you have a revitalizing homemade skin treatment. Here is just one of Ellie's face-saving recipes; tempt your skin to eat it up.

Ellie's Berry Beautifying Facial Scrub

$1/2$ cup cucumber, peeled and
   chopped (refresher)
6 large strawberries, hulled
   (cleanser, conditioner)
1 tablespoon baking soda
   (cleanser)
2 whole eggs (toner, binder)
2 tablespoons yogurt
   (conditioner)
$2/3$ cup ground almonds
   (exfoliant)

1. In a blender, puree the cucumber and strawberries.
2. Add baking soda, eggs, and yogurt. Blend on medium low for twenty seconds.
3. Add almonds, and blend for two minutes on pulse setting.

Apply the mixture in a gentle circular motion to a moistened face, keeping it away from the delicate under eye area. Make certain not to rub too forcefully as excessive pressure may irritate the skin. Leave the scrub on your face for about five minutes. Rinse off with warm water and again with cold water to close the pores.

Blot your skin dry and follow up with a cleanser or a mild floral water, such as rose or orange blossom, applied with a cotton ball. This berry scrub can be stored in the refrigerator for two days, after which time you want to discard (not eat) it.

During the summer months in particular, I generally try to deeply cleanse my face weekly with an aromatic facial steam. The process is quite simple. I place two cups of mixed garden herbs, such as lavender, lemon thyme, and a combination of mints, in two quarts of steaming water. I then drape a terry towel over my head to trap the steam, keeping my face about twelve inches from the water.

Once the steaming is complete, which takes about five minutes, I follow up with a yogurt masque (plain, never prune whip!) for another five minutes. I apply a thin layer of yogurt to my face and neck, avoiding the sensitive under-eye area. After I rinse off the yogurt with twenty splashes of warm water, I blot my skin with a cotton ball that

▼

has been moistened with Kiehl's Rosewater Facial Freshener-Toner or Orange Blossom Water from L'Occitane.

Or I might follow up the yogurt masque with a mint astringent that I make from a blend of mints from the garden. For this facial refresher, I use:

4 tablespoons finely chopped mint
8 tablespoons cider vinegar
3 cups distilled water

I place the mint and vinegar in a lidded jar, cover it, and leave it to infuse for a week, after which I strain it and pour in the distilled water. I bottle the astringent and keep it tightly covered in the refrigerator, shaking it well before use. After a warm, long day in the garden, this mint-scented, cooling astringent is just what the skin doctor ordered.

ᵛ ᵛ ᵛ ᵛ ᵛ **TIP** ᵛ ᵛ ᵛ ᵛ ᵛ

You can make lavender oil from your own plants. When packaged in a decorative bottle and tied with a sprig of lavender, it makes a lovely gift. To make the oil, fill a clear glass jar with lavender flowers and leaves. Gently crush the herbs with a wooden spoon and pour in enough oil to cover the herbs. (I use olive oil because it has a long shelf life.) Cover the jar and place it in a sunny window. Then all you have to do is mix it every other day. After several weeks, strain the oil through cheesecloth, pressing the herbs against the cloth to release the essential oil. Pour into small, dark glass bottles and store in a dry, dark place. The oil should keep for up to a year.

FIVE
▽▽▽▽

Simple ... Safe ... Sage Advice

Gardening has obvious potential for all sorts of collisions and clashes with Mother Nature, whether it's a bug in your eye or a thorn in your side. In the event that you are bruised, blistered, bugged, or blemished while you play at the sport of gardening, try treating yourself with natural remedies, such as witch hazel, arnica salve, or tea tree oil.

Some natural treatments can be found right in the kitchen, such as honey, oatmeal, and garlic. Or you can easily grow aloe, which is highly therapeutic, on a sunny kitchen sill. Natural remedies also grow in your garden or even in your lawn unless your lawn resembles a putting green. Is there plantain leaf peeking through your grass?

If you're itching to know how to manage pollen or hot to cool sunburned skin, I've done some of the groundwork for you, having had my fair share of run-ins with Mother Nature. In fact, the emergency room at Fairview Hospital in Great Barrington, Massachusetts, has been my destination on more than one occasion. Several years ago, a spider bite caused my ankle to inflate like a small pink balloon, and not long ago, a swinging pine branch scratched my cornea. Both instances needed medical attention, but for the most part, considering the many years I've been poking around in the soil, I really can't complain.

When and if possible, providing I'm not compromising my health or safety, my choice for first aid comes from natural remedies rather than "chemical warfare." Many of these remedies are family solutions (many actually are solutions) passed on to me; others come from friends who, like me, prefer to treat the garden-variety of sores, scratches, and strains the natural way.

Allergies

Even if you suffer from allergies, you can garden without sneezing and wheezing the days away. Granted, a rich harvest of molds and pollens can be potent allergens if you suffer from hay fever or asthma; however, with some luck, as well as planning, you can garden without your nose running quicker than the rabbits that raid your vegetables.

Hay fever and other allergies are usually brought on by pollen, the fine material that serves as the host for plant sperm. The good news is that many of the ornamentals and vegetables popularly found in household gardens do not produce allergy-causing pollen. That's because these plants are insect-pollinated, and such pollen is not easily inhaled.

Wind and insects generally function as the most common agents for dispersing pollen. It's capricious Mother Nature that determines whether pollen reaches wind-pollinated plants such as trees, weeds, and grasses. If it does, these plants may reproduce—and in the process generate immense powdery pollen, the type humans easily inhale into their lungs.

Unlike wind-pollinated plants, which are at the whim of Mother Nature, insect-pollinated plants have evolved into efficient reproductive machines, attracting a wide range of pollinating partners enticed by the plants' appealing scent, nectar, or edible pollen. Partners include not only bees but ants, beetles, wasps, moths, birds (primarily hummingbirds), butterflies, and even bats and the occasional pint-sized mammals.

Working outdoors in your garden (where you're exposed to small, airborne pollens) makes you vulnerable to allergies. Pollens are seasonal: Trees start in early spring, grasses commence in the summer, and weeds continue into autumn. So the potential for exposure begins in early spring and lasts until you put your garden to bed in late fall. The peak season for hay fever, however, is June to August, when ragweed and grasses are in flower. Ragweed pollen is the most common hay fever trigger in the United States.

Molds and fungi, an additional source of hay fever allergens, are the second offender for allergic gardeners. A profusion of moisture and organic substances is the perfect stew for the growth of molds and fungi. These crude organisms emit allergenic spores that produce a mold spore count that is many times (a thousand is not uncommon) greater than pollen counts.

Molds flourish in greenhouses and in dark, rarely disturbed areas. Garages (which fall into this category because you probably have yet to clean it or have a garage sale) and sheds with gardening tools are two such spots. There's still more to the mold story: Rotting vegetation provides the most severe exposure to mold. Compost or piles of leaves can be an allergy time bomb.

So how do you cope with your symptoms without sacrificing your scented geraniums or any other blooming thing that causes your eyes to water or your nose to run? The first step is to minimize exposure to allergens. I realize this is easier said than done. For starters, to take action and reduce pollen exposure, you really have to be aware of the times when bad pollen takes hold.

The highest counts are encountered in the early morning and late afternoon, so it makes good garden sense to schedule your chores for midday (which means you have to apply lots of sunscreen). Moreover, wind-pollinated plants favor warm and breezy weather, at which time, not surprisingly, they prefer to release their pollen, so if the wind acts up and causes your allergy to act up, act smart and head for the house.

Another wise strategy to reduce pollen exposure is to ask someone to perform those duties most likely to produce allergens (raking the leaves, mowing the lawn, or turning the compost). (Obviously, that someone had better not be allergic!) If you can't find that "someone else," think about wearing a protective mask

(check the A. M. Leonard catalog) while you work.

On the topic of mowing, if you react negatively to grass pollen, lying on the lawn after it's had a haircut is not a smart move. It could really set your eyes and nose off and running.

According to Dr. Andrew Weil, author of *Natural Health, Natural Medicine* (Houghton Mifflin), a safe, natural alternative to prescription medications for hay fever is the stinging nettle plant *Urtica dioica*. Nettles, according to Weil, relieve hay fever symptoms quickly in most people, without toxicity, which certainly is a major plus.

As you may know all too well if you've ever brushed against it, stinging nettle, a common plant throughout the world, has stinging hairs that inject irritant chemicals under the skin with memorable and unpleasant results. I speak from experience having had my brush with the nettles that grow behind my woodland garden. However, when dried or cooked, nettles lose their sting and can be therapeutic.

Weil's advice: The best form of stinging nettle is a freeze-dried leaf extract sold in capsules. The dose is one or two capsules every two to four hours as needed to control symptoms.

In addition to nettles, Weil recommends quercetin, another natural product that, according to him, helps manage hay fever.

Quercetin is a bioflavonoid obtained from buckwheat and citrus fruits. It appears to stabilize the membranes of cells that release histamine, the mediator of pollen reactions. Unlike stinging nettles, quercetin's action is preventative rather than symptomatic, so the best way to use it, according to Dr. Weil, is to begin taking it a week or two before the expected onset of the pollen season, continuing until the end.

Some quercetin products (sold in natural food stores) contain the pure substance; others combine it with vitamin C and other bioflavonoids that may or may not enhance its effectiveness. Since pure quercetin powder (yellow) is insoluble in water, Weil recommends taking it in the form of a coated tablet. Take 400 milligrams twice a day, between meals, regularly during the allergy season.

You can also use peppermint oil for an effective steam inhalation to relieve sinuses clogged from an allergy attack. Peppermint acts as a decongestant, and the combination of the warm steam and the essential oil is doubly effective for opening up the sinuses. Because peppermint has a relaxing effect on many people, it can bring relief from headaches that result from allergies.

To use peppermint oil as a steam inhalation, pour a quart of boiling water into a heatproof bowl and add four drops of the oil. The dosage is small because peppermint oil is powerful and could potentially irritate your skin if too much is used.

You then want to create a tent over your head and the bowl with a terry towel. Breathe in the steam for five minutes, making certain to inhale through your nose to bring the steam up into your sinuses.

For eyes that are red and itchy, eyedrops can bring relief as can antihistamines, which control both eye and nasal symptoms. However, these drugs might make you feel drowsy or cause blurred vision, which is certainly not something you want if you're operating equipment such as a lawn mower, weed eater, or chain saw.

In addition, decongestant nasal sprays and antihistamines can irritate the nose and cause headaches. So you really should avoid overusing these sprays. In fact, too frequent use can cause "rebound congestion," irritating your nasal passages and making matters worse. Remember as well that antihistamines merely suppress the allergy expression; they do not alter the allergic process.

If you choose to take them, antihistamines ideally should be taken before symptoms develop. If you plan to work in the garden and you know you're very likely to get a noseful of something, take the antihistamine thirty minutes to an hour ahead of time.

According to a New England herbalist, who has been a source of worthwhile information over the years, a combination of nettles with dried mullein leaf also effectively relieves allergy symptoms. Mullein, which grows to majestic heights and is an attractive addition to the back of the garden or a naturalized setting, has traditionally been used as a tonic to soothe the respiratory tract and promote the expulsion of mucus from the lungs. Nettles have astringent properties that help dry excessive mucus.

During allergy season, drink a minimum of four glasses of mullein-nettle tea daily. To make this brew, bring one quart of water to a boil, turn off the heat, add three tablespoons each of mullein leaf and nettles. Then cover the liquid and let it steep for at least an hour, or preferably overnight.

Desensitizing allergy shots are yet another option to consider. These induce a gradual tolerance to inhaled allergens through injections containing increasing doses of allergen extracts. Although a more complicated and costly process than squirting medication into your eyes and nose, or taking it orally, desensitizing shots may have an advantage because they treat the *cause* and not just the symptoms.

However, shots are expensive, and unfortunately, the percentage of patients who experience satisfactory relief from symptoms after years of therapy is disappointingly low. Many people view immunotherapy as a last resort, since it requires several months of weekly shots followed by approximately a year and a half of monthly shots.

▽ ▽ ▽ ▽ ▽ **TIP** ▽ ▽ ▽ ▽ ▽

Edible flowers make pretty garnishes for soups, salads, and desserts. But do not experiment unless you're sure the flower is safe to eat. Many flowers are unhealthy or, worse, poisonous, including sweet peas, foxgloves, lily of the valley, to name a few. And of course, any flowers that are to be eaten should never be sprayed.

Blisters

Perhaps you've gripped the shovel or spade too hard for too long, or jammed your feet into work shoes that were not sufficiently broken in. Whatever the cause, the result is an annoying blister, your body's protest against too much friction.

Blisters are not likely to form where skin is easily movable, but usually form where skin does not yield easily, like the palm of your hands or soles of your feet. Whether the blister is large or small, your main concern should be preventing infection while it heals.

For a small blister, the wise approach is simply to protect it and let nature take its course, so to speak. The fluid will gradually be reabsorbed and the top skin (roof) will peel off as layers of new skin push up from beneath it. Doughnut-shaped bandages can surround the blistered area with a cushioned surface so that it can heal on its own and, most important, you can continue to garden.

If the blister is large and likely to break, try to drain it yourself. First, clean your hands thoroughly, then clean the area with soap and water. Using a needle that has been sterilized in a flame, puncture the blister's edge in several places. Be careful to leave the roof of the blister intact; this protective covering will help prevent infection. Press the blister gently with a sterile pad until all the fluid has drained out. Then apply an antiseptic, such as tea tree oil, and cover with sterile gauze. On the other hand (and hands are common spots for blisters), if the blister has already broken, clean the skin gently with soap and water and cover it with antiseptic and a sterile pad.

Tea tree oil is something you really should keep in your gardening survival kit. This strongly aromatic, pale yellow oil, with an odor similar to that of eucalyptus, is pressed from the leaves of the small myrtle-family tropical tree *Melaleuca alternifolia*, native to Australia. It's a powerful disinfectant that works well on minor cuts, scrapes, blisters, and fungal infections. Just make certain that the label says it's pure and that you use it very sparingly, since it's really quite potent. And be sure to keep it away from the eye area.

One defense against foot blisters is to wear socks, not just shoes, particularly during the warmer months when your feet swell and thus cause more friction in the shoe. To avoid foot blisters, on the heel, toes, or wherever, make certain your gardening footwear fits properly: It should neither slip around nor hug your feet too tightly.

Generally, when I wear my waterproof gardening shoes (which are not for doing strenuous chores that require good support and protection), I also wear a thin pair of cotton socks to keep blisters at bay. Although I love the idea of being able to easily slip out of my Frog Hoppers to sprinkle my feet, particularly in hot weather, I'm willing to sacrifice the cooling foot shower for blisterless tootsies.

▽ ▽ ▽ ▽ ▽   **TIP**   ▽ ▽ ▽ ▽ ▽

Advice on dandelions: If you can't beat them, eat them.

Dr. James Duke, Botanist

Bruises, Cuts, and Scrapes

Talk about a contact sport! Contact with the rough edges of stones, branches that scratch, or thorns that cut and scrape your skin—gardening can really leave its mark on you.

Hardly a weekend passes that I don't come in from the garden with some species of skin wound, be it a cut, bruise, or scratch that needs tending. Providing it's not serious, which it usually isn't, I apply some homeopathic salve or lotion, or a natural remedy from my kitchen cabinet, and I'm back in the garden without missing a beetle.

You really don't need a medical degree to tend to the garden variety of minor wounds. To treat a cut, for instance, once pressure has been applied and the bleeding stopped, wash the affected area with mild soap and water, or use hydrogen peroxide to kill any opportunistic bacteria. If you've been cut by a sharp, dirty object, such as the edge of a rusty tool (reason enough not to leave them out in the rain), naturally you want to make certain you have protection from tetanus, so check to find out if your shots are up to date.

An antibiotic ointment such as Bacitracin or Neosporin can help zap any lingering bacteria and keep new bacteria from gaining a strong-hold. After you clean the wound and apply the ointment, cover it with plastic bandages or gauze and tape. Of course, before chemical medicines were available, wounds and cuts were treated the old-fashioned way, with herbal kindness. To my knowledge, there wasn't any Bacitracin sold at the pharmacy in the Garden of Eden. Rumor has it that the resident couple who gardened there treated their cuts and scrapes with natural herbal dressings made from, for instance, goldenseal (one of nature's best antiseptics) mixed with water.

To treat a minor cut or wound this way, steep a heaping teaspoon of goldenseal powder (a highly useful component of the herbal medicine chest) in a pint of boiling water for twenty minutes and apply it to the cut. This effective disinfectant encourages formation of a crusty scab that protects the wound from further injury. You can also make a paste of goldenseal powder and olive oil and apply it directly on the wound.

As for bruises, they're caused by bleeding under the skin. (Maybe instead of hammering the stake to support your tomatoes, you hammered your thumb.) Blood coagulates beneath the surface of the skin causing the characteristic black-and-blue appearance. Bruises, though not life threatening, are best treated for, shall we say, cosmetic reasons, unless of course you're partial to a black-and-blue color scheme. Minor scrapes and cuts not only warrant cleaning, but in addition, you want to soothe the "ouch." So what might you find in your kitchen to soothe the discomfort resulting from bruises and abrasions?

Are you ready for this one? A banana; and I don't mean that you should eat it. In fact, I'm not even talking about the actual banana; I'm talking about the peel. Stinging, pain, and general discomfort from minor scrapes and scratches can be alleviated by applying the inner skin of a freshly peeled banana to the affected area.

Should you not have a banana waiting in the wings to serve as therapy, a raw potato cut into a thin slice and pressed against the abrasion or bruise gives similar relief. If you don't want to hold the potato slice in place indefinitely (translation: you're itching to get back into the garden), you can adhere it to your skin with gauze and tape.

In addition to banana and potato, there's yet another item in your kitchen pantry that can provide minor wound relief. Honey has antiseptic properties proven effective against organisms that cause infections. But, according to herbalists, it should be unprocessed honey (unheated and unfiltered), the most effective type for killing a wide range of germs. What to do with it? After washing the cut with soap and water, just dab raw honey into the wound, cover it with gauze (which you should change daily), and you're ready to head back to your honeysuckle.

Another natural remedy for bruise relief is a compress made by soaking a cotton cloth in a cup of cold water to which you have added two or three teaspoons of witch hazel. Witch hazel is a simple, all-purpose, old-fashioned product that's been used for generations. When distilled and combined with alcohol, the aromatic oil extracted from the bark of the witch hazel shrub makes a soothing and mildly astringent lotion. It's clean, fresh fragrance dissipates quickly after being applied to the skin, a characteristic appealing to many. And with only about 14 percent alcohol, the lotion is nondrying as well.

If you have adequate space—it will grow up to 16 feet tall and as wide—preferably in a moist, wooded area, witch hazel is a wonderful plant to cultivate because of its unique blooming timetable. After autumn winds have bared the trees, witch hazel is ablaze with threadlike, sweetly scented yellow flowers. Traditionally used by northern Native Americans to treat skin problems, the astringent bark of witch hazel is recognized in the United States *Pharmacopoeia*.

My favorite store-bought variety

is Thayers Original Witch Hazel with Aloe Vera, but you can also make your own witch hazel by adding one teaspoon of the granulated leaves to a cup of boiling water. Let the liquid cool before you apply it to the problem spot. Speaking of witch hazel, a few drops added to rose, orange, or lavender water makes an ideal after-gardening skin refresher for your face.

Another remedy I use for gardening-inflicted bruises is arnica salve, which I massage into the affected skin. This soothing liniment, with its pleasant smell, reduces pain and swelling and encourages healing. Besides healing bruises, arnica ointment or lotion is also effective for relieving minor muscle soreness due to overexertion. One of my favorite brands of arnica is manufactured in France by Boiron and is readily available in natural health food stores. Though highly therapeutic for bruises and abrasions, you should not, however, apply arnica to broken skin, nor do you want to take it internally as a tincture or tea, since the plant is toxic when ingested.

I've also been advised by a nutritionist that if prone to excessive bruising, you may benefit from additional vitamin C in your diet. Vitamin C, as you probably know, is plentiful in foods such as citrus fruit, broccoli, and peppers, to name just a few sources. By maintaining capillary integrity, foods rich with vitamin C supposedly prevent bruising. Vitamin K, found in green leafy vegetables and soybeans, is also thought to prevent bruises because it helps blood to clot.

For nicks, cuts, and scrapes, aloe vera, a cactuslike member of the lily family, is also useful to have on hand. For topical use, aloe is sold as a gel, ointment, or spray. (Make sure to look for products containing 95 to 100 percent pure aloe.) Or you can use aloe gel from a plant grown at home (it needs sun), which is less costly and equally effective.

My aloe, which is now quite substantial and has given birth to numerous "youngsters" presently residing at other locations, sits in a big terra-cotta pot in my sun-drenched dining room (conveniently close to the kitchen if I burn myself while cooking). When I use it for a minor gardening-induced wound, I cut an inch-long piece (that's all you need) off the end of one of the lower leaves, slice it open lengthwise, and squeeze the gel onto the affected area. Aloe vera gel is good not only for burns and cuts but for blisters as well because its mildly astringent nature promotes tissue healing.

I've found that fresh aloe gel is much more potent than gel that has been stored and added to commercial preparations, which is exactly why I grow it at home. When using aloe, allow it to dry on your skin before you apply a bandage. Change the dressing every six to eight hours. It's always wise, however, to go easy the first time you try aloe, or any natural remedy for that matter, to make certain your skin does not react negatively.

Having mentioned several effective natural ways to manage minor cuts and abrasions, let me add a caveat: Any serious gardening-inflicted wounds should be brought to the attention of a medical professional. If you have a bruise that remains very painful for several days (you accidentally dug the spade into your foot instead of into the ground), there could be damage to underlying ligaments, muscles, tendons, or bones. Any bruise or cut that does not begin to show improvement within approximately a week should be seen by a healthcare practitioner.

Bugs in the Ear

There you are working happily in your garden, minding your business, when an insect crawls or flies into your ear. If you've had this problem, you know the buzz can sound frightening loud—not a mere song but a rock concert.

So what's the best way to evict the little fellow? Despite your natural response, refrain from putting your finger in your ear. If the insect has a stinger, the finger may provoke an attack. Or your finger might push it farther inside. Instead, pull the ear up and back and point it toward the sun or a bright light. Insects are attracted to light, so if you're lucky, it may crawl out.

If it's at home in your ear and refuses to vacate, obviously you have to take more aggressive action. Put several drops of mineral, baby, or vegetable oil in the ear canal to kill the insect and hope to float it out. Hold your head still, with the affected ear angled toward the ground. If all attempts to remove the insect fail

▽ ▽ ▽ ▽ ▽ **TIP** ▽ ▽ ▽ ▽ ▽

There's nothing quite like Bag Balm, the unique antiseptic made especially for cows but embraced by gardeners? That's correct; it's for chapped teats or superficial scratches and abrasions. According to the directions on the square green tin: "After each milking apply Bag Balm thoroughly and allow a coating to remain on the surface." Not only does this thick, petrolatum and lanolin-based salve (available in natural food stores, pharmacies, and garden centers) work for sore, chapped teats, but it's great for sore, chapped hands and scrapes as well. I use it as an antiseptic when I nick myself in the garden, for chapped lips, and for dry cuticles, too.

or if it stings you while inside your ear, seek medical assistance.

Bugs in the Eye ... Or Other Matter That Matters

In no time—in fact, in less than a blink of the eye—there's a bug in your eye. Talk about a nuisance! So what should you do to rid your eye of the little fellow when you can't blink him away?

According to my eye doctor, if an insect or a speck of dirt from the garden becomes lodged in your eye, flushing it out should be the first line of attack. If you can't bring on the tears to wash the eye out naturally while you're still in the garden, head for the house.

First and foremost, wash your hands. Then with your clean thumb and forefinger, push the eyelids away from the eyeball and wash out the foreign matter with cool or luke-warm water, or a saline solution used for contact lenses. Do not attempt to remove anything on the pupil or stuck in the white of the eye. You will only make matters worse by possibly scratching the covering of the eye (cornea).

If the object is on the inside corner of the lower lid, moisten a cotton swab or the tip of a twisted piece of tissue and touch it ever so lightly, but do not poke or prod. The object should cling to the swab or tissue. Some minor irritation is common after you have removed anything from the eye, so refrain from heading right back to the garden. Instead keep the eye closed to rest it, at least temporarily.

In general, unless you can successfully remove the harmless foreign object yourself, do not adopt a wait-and-see approach. Since your eyes are not only vulnerable but ever so valuable, playing doctor could very possibly cause irreparable damage. If you do wait, you might not see very well for quite a while, so contact your doctor soon. In the interim, before getting professional help, avoid touching or applying pressure to the eye, which will only cause the foreign matter to become further embedded.

To treat a scratched cornea, which can happen, for instance, when a branch ricochets (as it did for me), you should seek medical care as soon as possible. Your physician will, as mine did, medicate the eye with an antibiotic, which not only serves to heal the injury but numbs the pain. Generally, it's suggested that you wear a patch over the injured eye for several days to prevent the eye from blinking and thus irritating the cornea further. With proper medical attention, minor corneal scratches heal in several days.

The very important lesson I learned from the bough that

▽ ▽ ▽ ▽ ▽ **TIP** ▽ ▽ ▽ ▽ ▽

When you perspire profusely, not only do eyeglasses fog up, but they can slid off your nose and land in the soil, particularly when you work with your head lowered. To keep glasses from slipping and sliding, wear an eyeglass fastener (lasso) around your neck.

boomeranged was to always wear protective glasses when doing any garden work that could possibly compromise your eyes, such as pruning branches, pulling down vines, or cutting down overgrowth.

One more note about eye protection: Whether you wear contact lenses or not while gardening, touching your eyes with dirty fingers can invite infection.

Heat Exhaustion

If you garden maniacally and over-exert yourself (and neglect to drink fluids) during hot, humid weather, you could experience heat exhaustion, also known as heat prostration. As you may well know, sweating profusely depletes the body of vital fluids and minerals, which, if not replaced, can cause your muscles to cramp and complain.

That's why it's crucial to keep your body well hydrated. Drink plenty of water *before* thirst or weakness sets in. In fact, to fortify your-

self, particularly in the summer, always drink a tall glass of cool water before you head out to the garden. Then keep sipping (but not gulping) all day long.

Speaking of drinking, if you like to guzzle down iced tea or iced coffee while you garden, know that caffeine increases your vulnerability to heat exhaustion, as do alcohol, antihistamines, tranquilizers, and tricyclic antidepressants.

Besides muscular cramping, other symptoms of heat exhaustion include dizziness, headache, fatigue, and nausea. If you experience any of these symptoms, get out of the garden and into the house to cool off and rest.

To replenish lost fluids and electrolytes, drink water, juice, or a sports drink. The temperature of the drink should be cold but not iced. Cool salted water is also effective (one teaspoon of salt per quart of water); in fact, I find it every bit as beneficial as a commercial sports

▽ ▽ ▽ ▽ ▽ **TIP** ▽ ▽ ▽ ▽ ▽

Birds are natural insect predators and will help you battle the bugs, so welcome them into your yard. Some obvious ways are to provide berry-producing native shrubs and trees, feeders, houses, or nesting boxes for those arriving in the spring and a birdbath for those who welcome a cooling summer splash.

▼

drink. But whatever you drink, don't gulp; sip a little at a time.

To cool off further, you might take a cool bath or sponge yourself from head to toe with cool water, followed by a welcomed rest or nap. Only return to the garden if you're symptom-free and are "cool as a cucumber." If you do resume your work, be sure to wear a wide-brimmed hat, continue to drink plenty of fluids, and plant yourself in a shady spot.

Heat Rash

There are solutions (and some of them are actually solutions) to reduce discomfort from heat rash. If you are susceptible, the best way to prevent heat rash is to stay in cool, dry places during hot, humid days. I realize this is not exactly the advice an impassioned gardener wants to hear. So what else might you do? Schedule your gardening for the morning or late afternoon hours when the temperature is not quite as high and itch producing.

Also called prickly heat, heat rash is caused by obstruction of the sweat gland ducts (they become blocked and inflamed) and is characterized by small red and white itchy bumps. Although heat rash is hardly life-threatening, it's no fun to garden when your skin feels hot, irritated, and itchy.

▽ ▽ ▽ ▽ ▽ **TIP** ▽ ▽ ▽ ▽ ▽

If you like to garden with a can of soda at your side, be sure to check before you bring it to your mouth. Bees and hornets like soda, too; in fact, they're partial to all sweetened beverages.

To soothe the itch, you can topically apply aloe vera gel or calendula in various forms. This popular folk remedy derived from the bright yellow and orange flowers of the pot marigold (*Calendula officinalis*) is sold as an ingredient in herbal combination ointments, salves, lotions, and creams. Or you can make your own calendula oil quite simply from the plants you grow in your garden. (I love the bright orange accent that calendula flowers add to my herb garden all summer and into the fall.)

To make calendula oil, fill a clear glass jar with calendula petals. Gently crush them with a wooden spoon and pour in enough oil (olive oil has a long shelf life) to cover the petals. Cover the jar and place it in a sunny window, then shake it daily. After three or four weeks, strain the oil through cheesecloth, pressing the petals against the cloth to release the essential oil. Pour the oil into a dark glass jar and store it in a dry, dark place. You can massage the calendula oil directly on your skin, or you can add it to a skin-soothing bath.

Also effective for treating heat

rash is arrowroot powder (available in natural food stores), which you can sprinkle on the affected area. And the old potato trick comes in handy again. A slice of raw potato (the cooler, the more soothing) rubbed over the irritated skin will alleviate itching, as will a slice of fresh daikon radish.

Another remedy for relief from heat rash is a sponge bath made from ginger. For this soothing skin treatment, drop half a cup of freshly grated ginger (it increases circulation) into a quart of boiling water. But do not boil the ginger in the water, as it will lose its effectiveness. Let the mixture steep for five minutes, strain, and let the water cool. Sponge the ginger water onto the affected areas with a clean, soft cotton cloth, and let it dry.

One of my favorite bath products for cooling itchy skin is the Aveeno Bath Treatment (sold at pharmacies and other stores), which contains colloidal oatmeal. There's no measuring involved; all you have to do is open a packet and add it to the bath water. In fact, even if my skin is not irritated, a soak in this comforting oatmeal solution is always a good solution to a sweaty day gardening in the summer sun.

As for itching (and I don't mean to get into the garden), if it's generalized, whether from heat rash, bug bites, or whatever, a soak in a bath containing equal parts (one-half

> ▽ ▽ ▽ ▽ **TIP** ▽ ▽ ▽ ▽
>
> There's a heck of a lot of healing power in the tiny glass jar that holds Tiger Balm, a Chinese herbal remedy that smells not unlike Ben-Gay. For sore muscles, a little dab will do you. Just massage it into the painful spot and cover the area to trap the heat.

cup) of cornstarch combined with oatmeal can be soothing and effective.

Or you might try an anti-itch tactic that a gardening client of mine swears by: aloe vera in juice form. She spritzes Lily of the Desert Aloe Vera Juice, which is 99 percent certified organic aloe (sold at natural food stores), liberally on the affected areas several times a day and claims it works like magic for de-itching.

Insect Bites and Stings

Little bug bites can mean big trouble and major itching unless you know how to fight back. Here are a few bits and pieces of wisdom for when those little bites take pieces of you with them. Although getting bitten or stung is usually more annoying than dangerous, a few insects can make you ill if you happen to be allergic. Before you venture into the garden, you want to prepare for battle so that the troops don't lunch on you. A little knowledge is indeed an effective and beneficial natural repellent.

For starters, the difference between a bite or a sting has to do with the type of insect: hornets, yellow jackets, wasps, and bees, for instance, make their impression with a sting, whereas mosquitoes and ticks take a bite.

Mosquitoes are pesky little fellows, biting you and making you itch like crazy. These blood-sucking pests take only a minimal amount of blood but lots of the pleasure out of gardening. There's nothing quite as annoying as being trailed by a persistent army of mosquitos while you're trying to weed a bed. And, of course, if you've worked up a sweat, they like you all the more.

Since mosquito larvae hatch near or in stagnant water, take measures to eliminate these breeding grounds from your garden. Keep puddles from collecting by using an old broom to disperse any that collect after a rain.

Don't leave empty containers of any kind around the garden; turn them over so they will not fill up with rainwater. If you have a birdbath, you might consider installing a pump to constantly circulate the water; the birds will thank you for it, too. If a pump is not in your birdbath's future, be sure to empty and refill the water periodically. That does not mean monthly; weekly is

more like it. For a more substantial area of water, a pond for instance, I'm told by pond-proud pals that guppies eat the mosquito larvae, so get guppies!

There are all sorts of sprays and creams to discourage mosquitoes from making a feast of you, some far more effective than others. As you know, it's a matter of trial and error until you hit on one that will keep the little fellows from hitting on you.

I continue to rely on Avon's Skin-So-Soft products, the new Bug Guard in particular. It really does work for me, and I like the citronella scent, plus it's DEET-free. This product comes in a moisturizing lotion or a moisturizing sunblock spray (SPF 15), a welcome combination for any gardener.

If you prefer a totally natural repellent, try rubbing a bit of vinegar on your exposed skin. It really does keep the bugs from eating you alive; the smell of vinegar is less than alluring to them. (Romantically inclined husbands or significant others don't love it either!)

There are numerous chemical-free insect repellents worth checking out. One effective product is Bite Blocker by Consep (sold at nurseries), which contains plant oils, extracts, and derivatives as well as a skin moisturizer. I like it because it has a faint scent of geranium.

Another product that effectively keeps the bugs from bugging me (and it's 100 percent natural) is Lemongrass Insect Lotion from Burt's Bees. This potent but pleasant-smelling lotion contains grapeseed, lemongrass, citronella, and eucalyptus oils. Of all the products I've tried, this is one of the best.

Also very good, and 100 percent herbal as well, is Green Ban Double Strength, a product tested in the Australian rainforest ("when wildlife gets too wild") and sold at health food stores. This repellent comes in both regular formula and one for delicate skin. I like it because it not only repels insects, but also includes healing extracts and emollients to soothe insect bites and irritated skin.

Insects like sweet smells, so avoid wearing perfume, cologne, toilet water, or any fragrance products, or even an after-shave or hair conditioner. Just a dab of fragrance and the troops will swarm all over you.

This applies to a moisturizer for your face as well; opt for one that's unscented. One product that really works well for me is Beauty Fluid by Oil of Olay. This moisturizer offers light, sheer, greaseless protection (SPF 15) and is ideal for sensitive skin. Also make certain that the sunscreen you use is not scented if you want to keep the bugs in check as well as the rays.

If the mosquitoes land on you for lunch and leave their mark despite your efforts, wash any bites with unscented soap and cool water.

Avoid scratching, which can cause the toxins to spread. According to my dermatologist, applying ice immediately to the bite area not only soothes the irritated skin but prevents swelling as well.

One tried-and-true folk remedy effective for bites is baking soda. Add just enough water to the baking soda to make a paste, then apply it to the bite. This mixture not only helps relieve discomfort but decreases the reaction as well.

I've also found that applying tea tree oil, as quickly as possible, takes the itch away. Two drops of the oil mixed into a half cup of water is all you need. Then just blot it on the affected skin.

Did you know that meat tenderizer (like Ac'cent) contains an enzyme from papaya (papain) that neutralizes the venom in bee stings? For this remedy, make a paste with water as you would with the baking soda. Or skip the tenderizer and simply use fresh papaya (a more vegetarian approach). Mash a few tablespoons of the fruit and apply it to the irritated area: You can then snack on the remains; it's rich in digestive enzymes.

According to my friend Debbie, who's a never-ending source of natural survival tactics for gardening-related problems, plantain can take the pain out of a bite as well. Now if you've declared war on the weeds in your lawn, you've probably wiped out all the plantain, a broad-leafed herb of the plantago family with about 200 different species world-wide.

This very common plant grows in lawns (not lawns that resemble billiard tables) and has a long-standing reputation as a topically applied remedy for bites. To apply plantain, take a fresh leaf (look for the broad not narrow leaf variety) and pulverize it to break up the cells. Do not expect a thick liquid to ooze out the way gel flows from a pulverized aloe plant. When you take a fresh plantain leaf and crumble it up, it's moist like a damp cloth but not saturated with moisture.

Once you've crushed the plantain, apply the poultice directly to the bite. Use something to hold it in place, like a bandage or tape and gauze. In fact, Debbie's method is even more, shall we say, primitive. If she's working in the garden and is bitten by a pesty insect, she pulls the leaf right out of the grass, chews on it (it's not very tasty) to soften and break it up, then sticks it directly on her skin. That's what I call onsite bite combat. I've tried it and it works. But there is one caveat: Do not bite, chew, or swallow anything that grows on your lawn (or anyone else's lawn) if it has been treated with chemicals of any sort.

You might also want to check out an effective homeopathic gel called Sting Stop (available at pharmacies and manufactured by Boericke and Tafel). To relieve the discomfort of mosquito bites, apply the gel, which includes an infinitesimal amount of stinging nettle among its ingredients, to the affected areas and let it soak in.

Below are a few other ways to keep the bugs from bugging you—naturally.

► Consume more garlic to ward off garden pests. Just breathe on the critters and they'll be gone! Or perfume yourself with "eau de garlic": rub a clove on your neck or behind your ears where the bugs like to cozy up. Not only will they keep off, but they'll take off (so might friends and relatives).

► Give mosquitoes the brush-off by spritzing your arms, legs, and other exposed areas with citrus juice (lemon works well) mixed with water.

► Add marigolds, tansy, and garlic (natural bug repellents) to your garden beds.

► Ant bites, similar to bee stings, respond quickly to a paste of water and baking soda (sodium bicarbonate).

► Dab bites and stings with witch hazel, the colder the better. Keep a bottle in the refrigerator, just in case you need it.

▶ Oil of eucalyptus and essence of lavender reduce the sensation of heat resulting from an insect bite or sting. Just a dab will do it.

▶ For itch control, use a thick slice of onion as a poultice, holding it in place with a bandage. Or make a compress from grated onion and apply it to the bite site.

▶ Feverfew tea, made by infusing two tablespoons of the flower heads in a cup of boiling water, is an old country remedy for soothing bites and stings. Dab it generously on the affected areas and allow it to dry.

About 5 percent of people stung by insects are allergic. Symptoms include difficulty breathing and swallowing, weakness, and excessive swelling. In fact, for people sensitive to bee stings, one sting can become life-threatening. You should contact a physician or go to a hospital emergency room immediately if you experience any of the following: shortness of breath, wheezing, faintness, nausea, or vomiting.

If you do react to a sting in such a way, consult a doctor for a prescription for EpiPen, a spring-loaded device that triggers an anti-allergy injection when pressed against the skin. Knowing how to use it and having it at hand when needed make good gardening sense.

If you are stung by a honeybee (the only insect that actually leaves its stinger behind) here's how to remove it (there is a right and wrong way): Do not attempt to tweeze (or squeeze) the stinger because that could inject more venom into the wound. Instead, use a clean fingernail, a nail file, or a knife blade to flick it out.

After the stinger is removed, there are numerous remedies other than applying an antihistamine ointment. For starters, apply some ice for several minutes to keep the swelling down. Then you can use a paste of powdered meat tenderizer and water, or you can apply a cool and soothing compress of witch hazel.

Another option is to use a drop of peppermint oil on the sting site. Peppermint has anti-inflammatory and antiseptic properties, so it's an ideal choice. But you need very little as it is quite potent: A single drop applied two or three times a day is sufficient.

For wasps, if you see nests around the house (inside or outside), get rid of them. When I find one, instead of using chemicals, I use a broom handle to fell the nest. The best time to attack is dusk, because all the wasps will be back home (they have an early curfew) and will be disoriented by the dark.

If you do opt for the spray method (sprays shoot a stream about twenty feet), be ready to run quickly from the scene, not only to avoid getting stung, but equally important, to avoid breathing in the chemicals. You will kill all that the spray hits and any that escape will not come back to that particular nest.

As a final note: Walking barefoot on the grass might feel wonderful, but getting stung on the bottom of your foot does not. So keep your tootsies under wraps while you work in the garden.

"I continue to handpick the beetles, mosquitoes feast on me, birds eat the mosquitoes, something else eats the birds, and so on up and down the biotic pyramid."

WILLIAM LONGGOOD

Lyme Disease

On several occasions, I've come in from the garden only to discover a tick embedded in my skin, sucking away at my blood. Thankfully, not all ticks are created equal, which means not all are infected nor capable of transmitting the bacterial infection that causes Lyme disease. Thus far I've been spared, but that's partially because I'm careful about what I wear while I garden; I really cover up. I suppose I'm also more savvy about Lyme disease in general since a good friend and fellow gardener suffered severely from the ill-

ness when it went undiagnosed for too long.

As you might already know (let's hope not from personal experience), Lyme disease is transmitted by the bite of an infected deer tick (*Ixodes*), an insect about the size of the period at the end of this sentence. It's that miniscule until it bites you, and then it becomes engorged with blood. When this occurs, it can look much bigger, but it is still considerably smaller than a dog tick.

The tick prefers to feed on deer and other wild animals, but humans and domestic animals, such as cats and dogs, are by no means considered off-limits. Although the white-footed mouse is the primary reservoir of the bacterium that causes Lyme disease, they are not the only little guys who carry it. It can be brought onto your grounds and into your garden by chipmunks, squirrels, and birds. Because Lyme disease has been detected in some ground-feeding birds, you might not want to place birdfeeders and birdbaths very close to the house or where children play.

Lyme disease was first recognized in 1975 when a cluster of patients in Lyme, Connecticut, developed a strange type of arthritis. Since then, cases have been reported in almost every state and on every continent but Antarctica. In the United States, the heaviest concentrations of Lyme disease are in the Northeast, upper

Midwest, and Pacific Northwest. In fact, reports of Lyme disease have increased dramatically, and the disease has become an important public health problem.

The ticks that carry and transmit the disease-causing bacterium most commonly feed from May through August, exactly when the gardening season is in full bloom, so you really have to be on tick alert each and every day you garden.

Although the risk of exposure to ticks is greatest in the woods and fringe garden areas where there is deep grass or shrubby vegetation, ticks also may be carried by animals into lawns and garden beds. Because ticks live for two years, they have a considerable window of opportunity to infect not only wild and domestic animals but people, too.

Deer ticks cling to plants near the ground in brushy, wooded, or grassy places. Although they cannot fly or jump (like fleas), they certainly can (and do) climb onto animals and people who brush against the plants. Once they get onto the arms or legs of host animals, they attach themselves to a dark, moist part of the body.

Infection does not commence at the moment of attachment; the tick must be attached for at least twenty-four hours to pass on the bacterium. Therefore, removing the tick *promptly* will reduce your chances of being infected.

SYMPTOMS

Early stage:
In the first thirty days, you may experience flulike symptoms, including headache, fever, chills, malaise, swollen lymph nodes, and generalized aches and pains. In about 50 percent of cases, a skin rash develops, appearing as a circular red spot near the site of the tick bite. During several days or weeks, the rash usually expands while the center clears, giving a characteristic red bull's-eye appearance.

But remember, not all cases reveal a rash (my friend's did not), and many people never even see the tick, which drops off before the rash appears. Even if you've never had the doughnut-shaped rash, you can develop late-stage symptoms of Lyme disease.

Besides the circular rash, other skin signs can include burning or itching, hives, redness of the cheeks and under the eyes, as well as bloodshot eyes. The symptoms often go away untreated after a few weeks; however, the person remains infected. Without medical treatment, about half the infected people will get the rash again in other places on their bodies, and many will develop more serious problems later.

Later stage:
Left untreated, Lyme disease can lead to symptoms that reveal them-

selves months or, even worse, years after infection—although in many cases, symptoms show up within four to six weeks after the tick bite. Three major organ systems can be affected: the joints, nervous system, and heart. About 60 percent of people with untreated Lyme disease notice arthritic-like joint pain and swelling, particularly in large joints, such as the knee and hip. The arthritis can move from joint to joint and become chronic.

About 10 to 20 percent of people who do not get treatment develop nervous system problems. The most common symptoms are severe headache and stiff neck, facial paralysis or other cranial nerve palsies, and weakness or pain or both in their hands, arms, feet, or legs. These symptoms can last for weeks, often shifting from mild to severe and back again. Memory loss, mood changes, and difficulty concentrating can also result. Although uncommon, some people notice an irregular heartbeat.

Lyme disease can be easy to diagnose when someone gets the doughnut-shaped rash; obviously it is much more difficult to diagnose without the rash because the symptoms can mimic those of other ailments such as influenza or chronic fatigue syndrome. In fact, Lyme disease is called the "Great Masquerader." If you're pregnant and think you have been bitten by a deer tick, it's essential that you see your doctor, even in the absence of symptoms.

To help diagnose a potential case, doctors have laboratories test their patients' blood for antibodies to the Lyme disease bacterium. However, there is no test to date that is 100 percent accurate.

Antibiotic therapy is effective for treating Lyme, but according to my physician, one should wait until a doctor confirms a Lyme disease diagnosis before taking medications. Although some doctors do prescribe preventive antibiotic therapy before any symptoms of Lyme appear. Not only can taking antibiotics have side effects, which you obviously want to avoid if you can, but there is no evidence that taking the drugs immediately after a tick bite is better than waiting the few weeks for the results of a baseline and repeat blood test.

Once there is a positive diagnosis, treatment in most cases involves antibiotics given orally for at least two weeks. In severe cases, intravenous antibiotic therapy is administered, sometimes for several months or longer. Undiagnosed and untreated Lyme disease can result in serious multisystemic problems, so it is *crucial* to seek medical attention to begin treatment as early as possible.

According to a May 24, 1998, article that appeared in *The New York Times*, the government will soon consider a vaccine against Lyme disease. However, this vaccine will not prevent all Lyme disease and requires more than a year for immunity to build up. To date, the amount of booster shots needed has not been determined. According to Smith Kline Beecham, the company that developed the vaccine, called Lymerix, in a study of almost 11,000 adults, the vaccine was about 80 percent effective. But it took three doses to achieve maximum protection.

The best way to prevent Lyme disease is to know where the deer ticks are and avoid these places and to promptly remove the tick if you do get bitten. If you garden in a high-risk area, follow these tips.

▶ Wear long-sleeved shirts (tucked into pants), long pants (tucked into socks), and closed-toe shoes. The great "cover-up" might not be your choice of gardening attire, particularly when the heat's on, but covering up gives ticks less territory to land on.

▶ Wear white or tan clothing, as bright colors tend to attract insects. Light colors also allow you to better spot the tick on your clothes before it reaches your skin. Wear a hat for added protection.

▶ Do not assume that any insect repellent works on ticks. If you use a repellent, buy only EPA-approved products marked "effective against ticks." Read the labels carefully before application.

▶ Check your pet for ticks. Unattached ticks can transfer from your pet to you or a family member. Use flea and tick collars on pets and brush them carefully.

▶ Mow the weeds and grass around the house so that it's never too high. Remove leaves and clear the brush and tall grass at the edge of your garden.

▶ Remove any debris that might be a home for mice, chipmunks, and other tick-bearing animals. Remember, encouraging any wildlife to graze in your yard increases the chance that *Ixodes* ticks will be nearby.

▶ Keep woodpiles neat, off the ground, in a sunny area or under cover to keep dry.

After you come in from the garden, do a tick check slowly and carefully; don't rush through it. After you've done so, shower or bathe as soon as possible, checking again. Ticks take several hours to attach themselves to the skin; in the meantime, they can be washed away.

Their favorite places are on the legs, thighs, groin, in the armpits, along the hairline, and in or behind the ears. Since they are so tiny, use a magnifying glass to check out any new "freckles." Don't just check your skin; check your hair as well. Give it a good brushing out. If you can't manage a tick search on your own, get assistance, particularly for areas you are unable to see, such as your scalp.

Should you find a tick, remove it quickly. Use rounded-tip, fine-point tweezers. Cosmetic tweezers are not recommended because they crush the insect and leave it partly lodged in the skin. My tweezers, purchased at a medical supply store, have a magnifying glass attached. Grip the tick's body as close to the skin as possible. Do not use your fingers. Pull it straight out with gentle pressure.

Do not use alcohol, nail polish remover, or petroleum jelly to aid the process. You may inadvertently cause the tick to regurgitate, increasing your chance of getting the disease. Just pull gently until it releases, taking care not to crush its body.

Wash the bite area (as well as your hands) with soap and water and immediately put antiseptic, such as tea tree oil or alcohol, on the area. It's also important that you disinfect the tweezers. After doing so, put them away in your medicine cabinet so that you know exactly where they are in the event that you get bitten. Take my word for it: There's nothing more frustrating than finding a tick and not finding the tweezers!

Save the tick and take it with you to the doctor so it can be tested for pathogens. A laboratory can quickly tell if it is a female *Ixodes* tick and if it is engorged with blood (yours to be specific). If it is not an *Ixodes* tick, if it's male, or if the tick contains no blood, your chances of getting Lyme disease are extremely small, making further testing and treatment unnecessary.

If you have any problems extracting the tick, call your physician's office for further instructions or go to the emergency room of a nearby hospital. To secure more information about Lyme and other tick-borne diseases, you can reach the American Lyme Disease Foundation at 1-800-876-LYME.

"Better to hunt in fields, for health unbought, Than fee the doctor for a nauseous draught."

JOHN DRYDEN

Poison Ivy

The very best prevention for poison ivy is recognition. So remember the age-old saying, "Leaves of three, let it be." Regrettably, however, there are many plants with leaves of three, so it's best to become familiar (but not too familiar) with poison ivy (as well as oak and sumac) especially if you have a sensitivity to it and it happens to be growing on or around your property.

Remember, a cat or dog can transfer the ivy resin to you. Animals are not allergic to poison ivy, but if they happen upon it and some resin attaches to their fur, it can be transmitted to you when you pet them.

You can also have a wintertime reaction. Firewood is the culprit. If any ivy resins are on the logs, the smoke from a fire will throw them off, creating a situation that can be hazardous to a person sensitive to poison ivy. The same situation can occur if you burn debris such as leaves that contain poison ivy. So if you are sensitive, stay out of smoke's way.

If you do become contaminated, take action fast! Anything you do in the first five minutes with soap and water, or even just plain water, is going to beat what you do thirty minutes later. The most important aspect of treating poison ivy (oak or sumac) is to get the irritating plant oil off your skin *as soon as possible.*

If you head for the shower, make it a tepid or cool one. Warm or, still worse, hot water will open the pores and let the toxic oil seep into the skin. Use a strong grease-cutting soap, lathering two or three times, then rinsing it off.

If you're unaware that you've been contaminated, rest assured the telltale itchy rash will soon appear to let you know. Over-the-counter lotions containing calamine or zinc oxide can help relieve itching. One excellent product is Tecnu (sold at pharmacies). It will remove the oil from skin up to twenty-four hours after contact. If you are highly allergic to poison ivy or oak, you really should keep this product in your gardening first-aid kit. Tecnu is most effective when used within the first two hours after exposure, so have it close at hand, should you need it.

If you know you might come in contact with poison ivy, for instance when clearing a wooded area, you may want to apply Avon's Skin-So-Soft Ivy Block Lotion as a preventive medicine. Presently, this new, pre-exposure lotion is the only FDA-approved formula to help protect against poison ivy, oak, and sumac when applied before contact. The unique active ingredient, Bento-quatam, helps block allergenic, rash-causing plant oils from reaching the skin. Many of my friends swear by it.

Besides the old standbys for poison ivy relief (such as calamine lotion), there are also herbal remedies, many of which I've found to be very effective. For instance, a poultice of honey and powdered goldenseal, applied as a paste to the rash, clears up the condition in just a few days, providing it's fairly mild.

Applying goldenseal to a skin infection makes sense because of the herb's powerful antiseptic properties. Because goldenseal is highly astringent, it helps to dry and heal the weeping, oozing rash. Honey is the ideal medium to combine with powdered goldenseal because it soothes and has humectant properties that prevent the skin from becoming cracked and dry. For this poultice, mix equal parts of raw honey and goldenseal powder (available at natural food stores) into a paste. Spread it on the rash and cover it with a gauze bandage, which should be changed daily.

Another time-tested remedy is to treat the rash with a paste made from baking soda and water, not unlike what I suggested for treating insect bites. Not only is this particular paste soothing to irritated skin, but it may even prevent the rash from spreading. Once the paste has hardened, leave it on for thirty minutes. Then remove it with cool water and apply a thin layer of honey to the area. The honey will further soothe the skin as well as reduce swelling and prevent infection.

You can also soothe the itching and burning resulting from poison ivy with an oatmeal soak such as the one made by Aveeno, which works equally well for treating insect bites and prickly heat. In fact, Aveeno also makes an Anti-Itch Cream, enriched with natural oatmeal. Both products are highly effective.

You can also make your own oatmeal soak, as I do, to relieve the discomfort of poison ivy. Grind a cup of raw whole oats in a minifood processor or a coffee grinder until the oats resemble a fine flour. Then add the oats to a tepid bath and soak for at least ten minutes. Do not rinse off the film left from the oat water; leave it on your skin for soothing protection. Just lightly blot your skin dry.

In most cases, poison ivy and poison oak rashes will subside in about a week. If itching, redness, and swelling last longer than a week, if fever develops, or if the rash spreads to your eyes or mouth, consult a physician.

▽ ▽ ▽ ▽ ▽ **TIP** ▽ ▽ ▽ ▽ ▽

Even touching a shovel or hoe contaminated months earlier by poison sumac, oak, or ivy can cause a rash.

Sunburn

Selecting the correct SPF level for your sunscreen is every bit as important as knowing the pH level of your soil, believe me. In fact, you can correct the pH level far easier than you can correct sun-damaged skin. So unless you garden in total shade (which probably means you have a heck of a lot of hosta), you really have to be savvy about sun protection. Rays might be good for the garden, but not for the gardener's skin.

If you believe that you have a grace period in the sun before needing to cover up or if you think about using sunscreen only after your skin reddens or stings, think again. Besides increasing the risk of skin cancers, sun damages the skin by causing premature thinning and wrinkling. Helena Rubinstein, the cosmetic queen, said it most aptly "Sun ages you faster than bankruptcy!"

According to statistics from the National Cancer Institute, the incidence of melanoma (the most dangerous form of skin cancer) has grown by more than 140 percent in the last decade. So much for getting a healthy garden tan! You really can't be careful enough.

Years ago, before I truly understood how damaging sun can be, I would head for the garden with just the merest bit of suntan lotion applied fleetingly and sparingly to my face. Now, it's the big cover-up! Not only do I wear a full-spectrum sunscreen, but I wear a wide-brimmed hat or an enormous visor, even on cloudy days. I also cover my arms (despite the heat) with a long sleeved, lightweight cotton shirt. As for my legs, which in years past were not kept under wraps (and thus the reason for the brown sun spots), I generally wear a thin pair of cotton trousers, washed-out jeans, or denim overalls to keep my legs protected. Gone are the dog days of summer when I gardened in a pair of cut-offs and a skimpy tee shirt, or still worse, a bathing suit.

According to my dermatologist, who happens to be an avid Manhattan rooftop farmer, skin type determines just how much sunlight you can withstand without getting into trouble. Light-skinned individuals with light-colored eyes (especially those with red hair and freckling) run the greatest risk because they usually burn (not tan) when exposed to the sun. But don't be fooled. Dark-skinned people who tan easily can also do considerable damage to their skin because they withstand more sunlight without evoking any warning signal to tell them to seek shade.

Another skin risk factor, according to my dermatologist, is a family history of skin cancer. If you have a close relative with a skin malignancy, you should be particularly careful to protect your skin while you work in the garden. In addition, sores that won't heal or moles that enlarge or develop unusual borders or colors should be evaluated by a physician *immediately*. In fact, if you discover a marking anywhere on your body or notice something that looks different or has changed, do not hesitate to bring it to the attention of a dermatologist; early diagnosis is your best chance for curing cancers of the skin.

When choosing a sunblock, my doctor's advice is to look for products that have a minimum of SPF 15. Also, select one that offers broad-spectrum protection against both UVA (ultraviolet A) and UVB (ultraviolet B) rays. UVA penetrates the skin more deeply and is considered the chief culprit for wrinkling, leathering, and other aspects of photoaging. The latest studies show that UVA not only exacerbates UVB's carcinogenic effects but may directly induce some skin cancers, including melanomas. UVB radiation is more potent than UVA in producing sunburn. These rays are considered the main cause of basal and squamous cell carcinomas as well as a significant cause of melanoma.

The sun protection factor (SPF) stated on sunscreen products measures the length of time a product protects the skin from reddening due to UVB rays. For instance, if it takes twenty minutes without protection to begin reddening, using an SPF 15 sunscreen theoretically prevents reddening fifteen times longer—about five hours.

The Skin Cancer Foundation, an excellent resource for brochures, books, manuals, and audiovisual material, recommends SPFs of at least 15, which block 93 percent of UVB. While SPFs higher than 30 block only 4 percent more UVB, they may be advisable for sun-sensitive individuals, skin cancer patients, and people at high risk of developing skin cancer. They also allow some margin for error if too little sunscreen is applied.

While SPF is the universal measurement of UVB protection, no comparable standard exists for UVA. Scientists worldwide are working to develop a standardized testing and certification method to measure UVA protection.

According to the Skin Cancer Foundation, broad-spectrum protection is what you should look for in a product. The phrase indicates that a product shields against UVA as well as UVB. It does not guarantee protection against all UVA wavelengths, however. Most broad-spectrum sunscreens and sunblocks with an SPF of 15 or higher do a good job against UVB and short UVA rays; if they also contain avobenzone, zinc oxide, or titanium dioxide, they should be effective against the entire UVA spectrum.

A new micronized, transparent form of zinc oxide (Z-Cote) has been developed by Dr. Mark Mitchnick, medical director of SunSmart, Inc., a company in Wainscott, New York. Z-Cote has been incorporated into many sun protection products such as Oil of Olay's Daily Protectant UV Moisturizer (SPF 15), which I recommended earlier. It's also found in Nu Skin's nonirritating Sunright line, which I like a great deal. Unlike many sunscreens that I've tested, Nu Skin products absorb quickly and completely and leave no sticky residue.

Avon Sun (SPF 15 or 30), recommended by the Skin Cancer Foundation, delivers full-spectrum protection and is another favorite of mine, not only because it's oil-free, PABA-free, lanolin free, and hypoallergenic, but because it has been fragrance-screened for sensitive skin, which is very important to me.

If you take certain medications and garden on a sunny day, the medication (either taken orally or applied to the skin) can turn even brief sun exposure into a bad burn or uncomfortable rash. Sun poisoning due to medication is common with some sulfa-based medications, such as certain antibiotics and diuretics (water pills). Some prescription acne medications can also have this sensitizing effect and require avoiding the sun. That's why it's always important to inquire about possible sun reactions if you are taking any medication and plan to garden. Your doctor and pharmacist can answer questions regarding sun-drug interactions.

Ironically, some sunblocking lotions can cause a rash due to a sun-induced allergy to the chemical PABA. In fact, according to my dermatologist, 10 percent of people are allergic to PABA and thus should wear PABA-free products. But that's no longer difficult to do; major American cosmetic and drug compa-nies now offer products for sun protection that are not only PABA-free but fragrance free as well. The Skin Cancer Foundation can provide a list of the products to which they've given their Seal of Recommendation.

If you develop an allergy to a sunscreen, keep testing products until you find one that is well-absorbed, does not cause skin allergies, and has the right texture for you. It might take a bit of trial and error, but it's worth the expense and effort. If your skin is sensitive, before applying the sunscreen to your entire face, apply the product instead to a very small area. Take note of how your skin reacts. If all goes well, go for it!

Water-resistance is also important as you don't want to perspire or hose off your protection. Don't assume that after you apply a water-resistant

▽ ▽ ▽ ▽ ▽ **TIP** ▽ ▽ ▽ ▽ ▽

Lips get sunburned, too. Cover them with a protective cream made especially for lips, such as Kiehl's Lip Balm #1, a moisturizing, soothing treatment for dry lips, made with oils and sunscreen agents. Another product that works well is Burt's Beeswax Lip Balm, which contains an assortment of healing ingredients such as sweet almond oil, lanolin, Vitamin E, peppermint oil, and naturally . . . beeswax.

or waterproof product in the morning, you're done. No matter how waterproof a sunscreen claims to be, it rubs off when you wipe the sweat from your brow. As labels often indicate, even waterproof products should be reapplied often.

Perfumes can also cause sun reactions. Take my word for it, do not wear Shalimar while you garden. There I was happily weeding away (years before I knew better), only to end up with hideous, red, itchy blotches behind my ears—as well as a battalion of gnats.

In fact, wearing products with fragrance of any kind while you garden, even a skin moisturizer or hair spray, isn't smart. Not only do perfumes attract insects, but some, like Shalimar, contain bergamot, an essential oil that increases photosensitivity. Bergamot gives Earl Grey tea its distinctive scent and humans a distinctive rash when it's applied to the skin exposed to the sun.

What else can you do to limit your risk of sun exposure without limiting your time and pleasure in the garden? A broad-brimmed hat (it also keeps your head cool) is using your head, as is working in a shaded, or at least semishaded, area during the hours of most intense sunlight (usually between 10 A.M. and 2 P.M.). This is one sun-smart strategy I attempt to follow, although I can't say it's always easy to manage. Instead of working, for instance, in

the perennial border next to the garage, which is sun-drenched from noon until two in the afternoon, I tend to that bed early in the day or after three o'clock.

Timing your work to avoid overexposure to the sun can really make a difference, not only for the health and safety of your skin. Working in the heat of the day in your sunniest areas can also be more debilitating. Opt to work on beds that are either in partial or full shade when the sun is hottest. Then you won't waste precious energy by sweating it away.

Below are some additional hints for gardening smart in the sun.

► Apply sunscreen at least thirty minutes before going into the garden. It takes this long for the active ingredients in sunscreen to bind with your skin cells. Make applying sunscreen part of your morning routine, like brushing your teeth. If you moisturize your face, apply the moisturizer first, followed by the sunscreen. Or apply a moisturizer with a sunscreen.

► Don't be stingy about application; apply sunscreen liberally and evenly to all exposed areas. Not using enough will reduce the product's SPF and the protection you get. How much is enough? A lot more than you might think. Figure on at least a tablespoon for each limb. Be sure to spread it evenly and rub it in thoroughly for maximum protection.

▶ Reapply at least every two hours (no matter what the label says) if some of the product has been removed while sweating.

▶ To be safe (not sorry), replace opened tubes of sunscreens that have been sitting on the shelf for several years. They can last for about three years, but they may degrade and become less effective. Clues are a change in odor or consistency. When in doubt, toss it out!

▶ Zinc oxide (the white stuff lifeguards put on their lips) provides double insurance for your nose and other burn-prone areas, such as the tops of your ears.

▶ Lips have no pigmentation and are easily sun damaged, so apply a lip balm with an SPF of at least 15. (I like the one from Nu Skin because of its cooling effect.)

▶ Wear long-sleeved shirts and long pants. The more tightly woven the fabric and the darker the colors, the more protection you get. (Unfortunately, bugs and bees are attracted to dark colors.) If you can see light through a fabric, UV rays can get through, too.

▶ Water makes fabrics more translucent, so don't hose down your T-shirt.

▶ A broad-brimmed hat goes a long way toward preventing skin cancer in often-exposed areas like the neck, ears, scalp, and face. Opt for a three-inch brim that extends all around the hat. (Baseball caps and visors shade the face but leave neck and ears exposed.) W. Atlee Burpee carries a cool and comfortable wide-brimmed hat that I like because of the ventilation holes in the crown. Another hat that caught my attention (actually, you can't help noticing it, but that's exactly what makes it so perfect) is the Halo, manufactured by The Topsy Tail Company. This collapsible, water-resistant hat has a five-inch brim that protects my face, neck, and shoulders from sun and light summer showers.

▶ If you want to keep sunscreen from getting in your eyes, form a protective barrier by drawing half circles above the eyebrows with a waxy sunscreen stick, such as Neutrogena Sunblock Stick (available at drug stores) or Facial Sun Stick sold through the Body Shop. You can also apply these clear products all over your face. The best part about stick application is that your hands never get greasy.

▶ UV-blocking sunglasses with wraparound or large frames protect your eyelids and the sensitive skin around your eyes, common sites for skin cancer and sun-induced aging. Sunglasses also help reduce the risk of cataracts later in life.

If after a day in the garden your skin, despite your efforts, is a hue similar to your salmon impatiens (which are wise and choose not to sunbathe), you have taken in far more than a healthy dose of rays. You must cool your skin down—and rethink your approach to sun protection. When you're feeling the sensation of heat, your skin is continuing to burn.

My grandmother's remedy for sunburn (she lived to ninety-six and gardened well into her eighties) was black tea. I still have visions of her lying on her very uncomfortable Victorian-style sofa, wet tea bags applied to her face. Or she would add a quart of strong black tea to a bathtub of lukewarm water. After a fifteen-minute soak, she would blot her skin dry and then apply aloe vera gel from a plant she grew (she was my aloe inspiration) on her kitchen windowsill. According to her, the tea soak, followed by the aloe vera, kept her skin from peeling.

Another remedy for sunburn is to add two cups of apple cider vinegar (if you can manage the smell) to a tepid bath and soak for about fifteen minutes. After the bath, spray your sunburned skin every hour with a mixture of three-quarters cup of vinegar mixed with one-quarter cup of pure aloe vera juice.

After a day or two, when the burned area is no longer hot to the touch, you can then apply a salve or ointment containing calendula, comfrey, St. John's Wort, or echinacea, all of which will aid in healing the skin and preventing infection. But remember, every moment in the sun adds up, accumulating like money in the bank. The payoff is damage to the skin. So when you garden, apply sunscreen and sun sense.

"There can be no other occupation like gardening in which, if you were to creep up behind someone at their work, you would find them smiling."
MIRABEL OSLER

Thorn Removal

Getting stuck with a thorn is one thing, having it stick around inside your finger, or wherever, is another thing. Thorns are annoying and belong on rose bushes, not in gardeners.

To remove one, do what you would for a splinter: Grasp the end of the thorn with sterilized tweezers and gently pull it out. If the thorn is embedded in your skin, clean a needle with alcohol and make a small hole in the skin over the end of the thorn. Then lift the thorn with the tip of the needle until it can be grasped with the tweezers and pulled out. Once you have removed the thorn, you should disinfect the area by washing it with soap and water, after which the area should be protected with an antiseptic such as tea tree oil.

For the sake of keeping infection at bay, not only should the tweezer be sterilized but your hands should be washed beforehand. If you're planning to continue to work in the garden after "surgery" has been performed, cover the area with a bandage so that no dirt can enter the wound.

To avoid getting stuck in the first place, when pruning roses or clear-ing brush, protect your arms and hands with thorn sleeves or gauntlet gloves. I purchased mine through the Kinsman Company Gardener's catalog, which is chock full of gardening goodies.

"There is no "The End" to be written, neither can you, like an architect, engrave in stone the day the garden was finished; a painter can frame his picture, a composer notate his coda, but a garden is always on the move."

MIRABEL OSLER

PRODUCT RESOURCES

Aēsop
1-888-223-2750

Avon
1-800-FOR-AVON

The Body Shop
1-800-BODYSHOP
1-800-263-9746

The Bugchaser
1-800-969-9909

Burt's Bees
919-510-8720

Crabtree & Evelyn
1-800-CRABTREE

Devon Lake Enterprises (Clawdia)
634 Clarks Tract
Keswick, VA 22947
804-293-6689

Dr. Hauschka Cosmetics
1-800-247-9907

Kiehl's
1-800-KIEHLS-1

Kinsman Company
Gardener's Catalog
1-800-733-4146

L'Occitane en Provence
1-888-623-2880

L. L. Bean
Freeport, Maine 04033
1-800-341-4341

Nu Skin
1-800-487-1500

Nutri Power High Energy Bar
1-800-541-4720

The Skin Cancer Foundation
245 Fifth Avenue
Suite 1403
New York, NY 10016
212-725-5751

Step 2 Corporation
1-800-347-8372

Sun Feather Handcrafted
1-800-771-7627

Topsy Tail Company
214-691-1630

W. Atlee Burpee
1-800-888-1447

Well-Sweep Herb Farm
205 Mt. Bethel Road
Port Murray, NJ 07865
908-852-5390

Wonder Gloves
1-888-660-8511

The following mail-order companies carry ergonomic gardening tools:

A. M. Leonard
1-800-543-8955

Brookstone Hard-to-Find Tools
1-800-926-7000

Earth Made
1-800-843-1819

Gardener's Supply
1-800-863-1700

Langenbach
1-800-362-1991

One to Grow On
1-888-383-2240

Plow & Hearth
1-800-627-1712

Walt Nicke's Garden Talk
978-887-3388

INDEX
▼▼▼▼▼▼

Numbers in boldface refer to boxed text.